WILDFLOWERS
of the NORTHERN PLAINS and BLACK HILLS

Theodore Van Bruggen
Biology Department
University of South Dakota

NATIONAL
PARK
SERVICE

Department
of the Interior

2nd Edition
1976
Library of Congress Catalog Card Number: 79-126933

International Standard Book Number: 0-912410-04-3 Softcover
0-912410-03-5 Hardcover

Published by the Badlands Natural History Association in cooperation with
the National Park Service, U.S. Department of the Interior

Bulletin No. 3

FOREWORD

For people who enjoy life and the discovery of its various forms, there are many ways to begin an exploration. Sometimes the light from an outside source sheds the needed inspiration or guidance which can make the exploration more worthwhile. Those interested in life in the form of wildflowers of the northern plains and Black Hills have not had the help of a color-illustrated, popular work on this subject until now. I am very pleased that Dr. Theodore Van Bruggen was able to fill this void by authoring this book.

Dr. Van Bruggen, who is a professor at the University of South Dakota, is a well-known plant taxonomist and biologist and is a recognized authority on the flora of the northern plains and Black Hills. He co-authored "A Check List of the Vascular Plants of South Dakota" in 1959 and is presently working on a technical key for all vascular plants in South Dakota.

I hope that this publication may encourage your interest and curiosity so that you will be led to many discoveries in this rich area.

Cecil D. Lewis, Jr.
Former Superintendent, Badlands National Monument

ACKNOWLEDGMENTS

For a number of years, I have had an interest in the flora of South Dakota and have had a hobby of photographing plants for university classes in biology. Three years ago Mr. John W. Stockert, Interpretive Specialist at Badlands National Monument, acquainted me with a wildflower publication that he and his wife had just completed on the Grand Canyon of the Colorado River. His enthusiasm and expertise gave me the incentive to write this volume. I am particularly grateful for his guidance in layout, choice of photographs, and editing. He also aided much in selecting the most appropriate common name for each plant.

My deep appreciation and gratitude is extended to Dr. Norman H. Russell for the privilege and honor of using his very appropriate poem.

I also wish to thank Miss Susan J. Sindt, 1970 seasonal naturalist, Badlands National Monument; and Mr. George A. Fisher, Jr., former Administrative Officer, Badlands National Monument; who unselfishly contributed much technical assistance in critically reviewing the manuscript.

To Mrs. Clarence N. Kravig of Lead, South Dakota, Mr. George E. Kellogg of Rapid City, South Dakota, and Mr. Stockert, I am indebted for their special interest and generosity in supplying a large portion of the photographs.

Finally, I wish to give recognition to my wife, Gerry, who has accompanied me on many collecting trips in the northern plains and Black Hills. Her patience, interest, and help is much appreciated.

Theodore Van Bruggen

November 6, 1970

INTRODUCTION

By a conservative estimate, there are about 2,000 species of flowering plants native to the northern plains and Black Hills of the United States. Of these, 230 have been chosen as characteristic representatives for this book. This region, roughly 600 miles square, includes the western parts of Minnesota and Iowa, all of North and South Dakota and Nebraska, and the eastern parts of Montana and Wyoming. The area lies within the large geographic sector known as the Grassland Province which extends as a broad, north-south belt through mid continent from Alberta to Texas. It has a climate of hot, semi-humid to dry summers and cold winters.

Variations in temperature and rainfall profoundly affect the establishment and distribution of plants and animals. In extreme situations, temperatures in the northern plains and Black Hills vary from 116 degrees to more than 40 degrees below zero Fahrenheit! The average yearly precipitation ranges from about 14 inches in the western plains to nearly 29 inches in the eastern part; the northern Black Hills may receive about 30 inches. In the plains, more than ½ of this precipitation falls just before and during the growing season.

As rainfall increases from the Rockies eastward, the vegetation of the Great Plains changes from shortgrass prairie in the west to mixedgrass prairie through the middle and to tallgrass prairie in the east. Occasional stands of native, deciduous forests occur in the eastern part of the grassland, and further east the tallgrass prairie ultimately gives way to deciduous forests. Because of extensive cultivation, the interlacing of prairie and forest along the eastern edge of the grassland is hard to see. Only in protected areas, such as in some ravines and along stream courses, are vestiges of native forests found.

The Black Hills of South Dakota and Wyoming form a striking contrast within the Grassland Province. The mountainous habitat with its greater precipitation offers many species not found in the surrounding prairie. Almost ¼ of these species are also widespread in the Rocky Mountains which are more than 300 miles west.

For easy identification, the wildflowers in this volume are grouped according to color with the yellows first, then the whites, reds, and blues. In some instances, particularly between the red and blue sections, it was difficult to place certain species which vary widely in color or which may appear to some individuals to be more like one color but to others more like another. If there is question as to which section a flower belongs, please check more than one section. Within each of the four color groups, the arrangement is according to blooming season with those flowering earliest shown first.

Among other things, the descriptions for each plant include the approximate blooming dates, general habitat, type of plant, and an x-factor. Flowering dates vary, depending on the terrain slope, moisture availability, the elevation of the plant if in the Black Hills, and to a lesser degree, the latitude and exposure of the site where the plant grows. The captions also include, if known, some pioneer and Indian uses. An x-factor is shown under each description to indicate how much smaller or larger the illustration is compared to the actual flower.

If you are interested in hunting for wildflowers, you may not have to go any further than the right-of-way of a nearby road or railway. However, to experience a large expanse of native prairie, more effort may be necessary, as there are only a few such areas remaining. The land can adjust on its own quite delicately to the vagaries of the climate, but man's presence has brought a new element which is sometimes felt in the harshest of terms. Eroded gullies, past dust storms, overgrazing, and abandoned farmsteads attest to man's unwillingness or inability to live within the laws of nature. Extensive cultivation, draining potholes, cutting timber, and other acts of man have made many native plants of the high plains extremely rare.

Fortunately, some tracts of native prairie have purposely been protected and preserved. These areas, though some are not large, include Agate Fossil Beds National Monument, Nebraska; Badlands National Monument, South Dakota; Cayler Prairie near Lake Park in northwest Iowa; Custer Battlefield National Monument, Montana; Pipestone National Monument, Minnesota; Sieche Hollow State Park near Sisseton, South Dakota; and Theodore Roosevelt National Memorial Park, North Dakota. All are excellent for viewing many of the flowers in this book. Aesthetically valuable, these lands also help preserve plant and animal life and serve as a yardstick for measuring how best to use other prairie areas.

There is not a best time to see the prairie. Late spring and late summer, perhaps, bring the more showy displays of wildflowers. But any time is a good time to visit. The ways in which seeds and spores are distributed, how rain and snow are held in the topsoil, and how the gradual decay of plant and animal remains enrich the land can all be noticed when the prairie is not in bloom.

Native plants should never be wantonly collected or destroyed. Many are transplanted with success, but certain species — and they usually are rare — need environmental conditions that are difficult or impossible to duplicate in gardens or lawns. Orchids, lilies, gentians, and evening-primroses are among many in this category. On the other hand, many asters, penstemons, and cacti grow easily when transplanted.

Here is a suggestion. Do what many who are sensitive to the preciousness of our prairies and forests have done. Go hunting with a camera! Many excellent inexpensive single-lens-reflex cameras are available. With a little practice and patience, a trip to the prairie will be highly rewarding and may be relived many times.

SKUNKBUSH SUMAC

Rhus aromatica   Cashew Family   April – May

This shrub grows 4 to 6 feet high on
hillsides, in ravine breaks, and at the edges
of bluffs and buttes in the prairie. The
vegetation is ill-smelling, hence the common
name. Tiny, yellowish flowers begin blooming
in clusters along the small, woody branches
shortly before the three-lobed, hairy leaves
appear. Quarter-inch, red fruits ripen in late
June and July. Plains Indians used the branches
in basketry and ate the berries. Though closely
related to Poison-ivy (*R. radicans*), this sumac
is not poisonous.

4x   Stockert photo

Yellow Flowers

MISSOURI GOOSEBERRY
Ribes missouriense   Saxifrage Family   April – May

Typical of wooded hillsides and ravines, this shrub has numerous, woody
stems which grow 4 to 5 feet tall. They are irregular and lax, having
needle-sharp spines. The delicate flowers vary from white to yellow and
are sometimes tinged with purple. They usually bloom before most leaves
come out. Fruits ripen to deep purple from late June into September.
Indians relished the gooseberry, eating the fruits raw or cooking them
with grains and meat.

3/4x   Van Bruggen photo

PRAIRIE GOLDENPEA
Thermopsis rhombifolia   Legume Family   April – July

This perennial herb grows on open banks and eroded slopes to about a
foot tall. The showy flowers typify the flower structure of the Legume
Family. The upright petal is called tha banner, and the two side petals
are called wings. The remaining two, lower, fused petals form the keel.
The keel contains 10 stamens and the ovary which forms a small, curved
seedpod. Indians burned the nearly dried flowers and confined the smoke
to arms or legs that suffered from rheumatism.

1/3x Stockert photo

5

NUTTALL VIOLET
Viola nuttallii   Violet Family   April – June

The name of this perennial commemorates Thomas
Nuttall, a noted botanical explorer of the western
plains in the early 1800's. This is one of the few
violets of temperate North America with lance-shaped
leaves. The short-stemmed plant, less than 6 inches
tall, bears yellow flowers with brown or purple lines
deep in their throats. The herb is inconspicuous
in its preferred habitat of prairie sod. However, as
it blooms before other plants gain much growth, its
flowers make it more noticeable.

2x   Stockert photo

SAGEBRUSH BUTTERCUP
Ranunculus glaberrimus   Buttercup Family   April – June

The five-petaled, waxy flowers of this meadow
perennial typify the some two dozen buttercup
species growing in the high plains and Black Hills.
Usually found in marshy or moist, wooded places,
most have dissected leaves. The fruit resembles
a strawberry, with many one-seeded fruits, called
achenes, crowded on a receptacle. This herb has
a toxic compound that may produce ulcers in
grazing animals.

3x   Stockert photo

LEAFY MUSINEON
Musineon divaricatum   Parsley Family   April – June

This native herb of the northern plains was called
Wild Parsley by pioneers because of its similarity to
the cultivated form. The stem, growing from a thick,
perennial root, is short with spreading leaves that are
compounded into many segments. The small, yellow
flowers are arranged in a tight umbel, an umbrella-like,
flower cluster with all the flower stalks originating
from one point. Each umbel is about 1 inch across.
The oval fruits have oil tubes which are characteristic
of the Parsley Family. The roots are bitter and
probably were not eaten by Indians except in
periods of famine.

1x   Stockert photo

COMMON DANDELION

Taraxacum officinale   Composite Family   April – Oct.

The nemesis of a weed-free lawn, Common Dandelion is
notorious for growing in places where it is not wanted.
A European native, it has invaded most of temperate
North America. It is a unique living organism to
biologists because it can set seed without pollination
or fertilization. This characteristic has developed
many forms that differ from each other in small but
significant ways. The dandelion is one of the highly
evolved members of the plant world. A prolonged warm
spell may cause the perennial herb to flower
during any "off season" month.

1/2x   Van Bruggen photo

GOLDEN CURRANT

Ribes odoratum   Saxifrage Family   mid April – June

This showy flower with a red center has a spicy odor.
Woody stems reach a height of 4 to 10 feet. The lack
of spines on these stems distinguishes the currants
from the gooseberries which also belong to the genus
Ribes. The small leaves of Golden Currant are deeply
three-lobed. Plants grow principally on rocky
hillsides and on north-facing slopes of ravines. The
berries which ripen in late June and July make
excellent jam and wine. Sioux Indians used the tart,
bluish-black currants in making pemmican. The shrub
is commonly grown as an ornamental in this region.

1x   Stockert photo

WAVYLEAF FALSE-DANDELION

Microseris cuspidata   Composite Family   late April – May

This herb, also called Prairie Dandelion, has flowers
that are quite similar to Common Dandelion (see
above) although this one has long, wavy-edged
leaves with a whitened line of hairs on each edge.
Lacking aboveground stems, the leaves are borne at
soil level. The flower heads, slightly broader than
those of Common Dandelion, are at the tops of leafless
stems called scapes, that are about 10 inches long.
Usually the blossoms are open only in the forenoon.
This perennial is a native in the north central
plains where it tends to grow in patches in moist prairies.

3x   Stockert photo

CLEFT GROMWELL
Lithospermum incisum   Borage Family   late April – June

The yellow flowers of this prairie herb are each about ½ inch long and are almost hidden by leaf-like bracts. The petals have a fringed or crinkled margin. The generic name *Lithospermum*, meaning "stoneseed," refers to the hard, whitened fruits that develop later. Plains Indians used the woody taproot for food and medicine. There is also a purple juice in the roots of this perennial and of a closely related species, Hoary Gromwell (*L. canescens*), which was used as a dye. Cleft Gromwell, also called Puccoon, is frequently found on prairies, especially in the western part of the plains.

1x   Stockert photo

LOUISIANA BLADDERPOD
Lesquerella ludoviciana   Mustard Family   late April – June

Each flower of this perennial has four, regular, yellow petals that form a cross; this is the typical petal arrangement of the Mustard Family. The spherical fruiting pods, almost ¼ inch in diameter, are topped with a short beak. The seeds within were occasionally used for food by prairie Indians. The stems, attaining a height of 12 inches or more, bear leaves that are spatula-shaped, with the widest part towards the tip. Animals generally avoid this herb when grazing. This is but one of a number of bladderpods that inhabit the prairies in dry, sandy areas.

3x   Stockert photo

COMMON LOUSEWORT
Pedicularis canadensis   Snapdragon Family   May – June

The common name comes from an old European belief that cattle grazing on the Old World species would get lice. Flowers are strongly two-lipped with two of the five united petals forming an arched top. Usually yellow, they are oftentimes tinged with red. Stems are short and plants are tufted from a rootstock. Often the roots are associated with the roots of other plants. Common in the Eastern United States, this herbaceous perennial reaches the eastern part of the high plains, particularly in low, moist prairie.

1x   Van Bruggen photo

SMALL-FLOWERED BUTTERCUP

Ranunculus abortivus   Buttercup Family   May

The yellow flowers of this buttercup are less
than ½ inch in diameter. During and after
flowering the stems of this plant elongate and
branch, reaching up to 18 inches tall. The
basal leaves are rounded in outline and the
stem leaves are deeply three or five-parted.
The fruiting heads are typical of the buttercup
family, having many achenes crowded on the
receptacle. The Small-Flowered Buttercup is
common in alluvial woods and thickets over
the eastern plains.

3x   Van Bruggen photo

YELLOW WATER CROWFOOT

Ranunculus flabellaris   Buttercup Family   May — June

The vegetative parts of this aquatic buttercup
are mostly below the water level. Leaves are
divided into many linear segments and even
the submersed ones effectively catch many of
the sun's rays for manufacturing food. The
Yellow Water Crowfoot grows in quiet water of
ponds and lakes throughout the northern plains.
Rooted in the mud, it grows in large patches
and forms an attractive appearance when in
flower. It reproduces by seeds, by fragments
that are carried by waterfowl, and by the
offshoots of the perennial roots.

1/6x   Van Bruggen photo

NARROW-LEAVED MUSINEON

Musineon tenuifolium   Parsley Family   May — June

This member of the parsley family is
relatively common in the Black Hills. It
grows in more rocky places than the Leafy
Musineon (see page 6.) It also lacks a main
stem above ground. The narrow, linearly
dissected leaves arise directly from the
root crown. Individual flowers, very small
and borne in tight clusters, may vary in
color from bright yellow to off-white.
Although bitter, the roots of this plant were
used as a survival food by American Indians
during harsh winters.

1/3x   Van Bruggen photo

BRITTLE PRICKLYPEAR

Opuntia fragilis   Cactus Family   May – July

This cactus is appropriately named, for the stems are fragile, breaking at the narrow point where they join each other. Such brittleness has great survival benefit because it enables the plant to reproduce vegetatively; the piece of broken stem simply roots in a new location. This is the only pricklypear in the northern plains that has cylindrical joints instead of flat ones. Because the succulent plants are small, they are difficult to find in the prairie grasslands except when the pale yellow to orange flowers are present. The fruits of this perennial are dry and not edible.

1x Stockert photo

WESTERN WALLFLOWER

Erysimum asperum   Mustard Family   May – July

The scientific name for the Mustard Family is *Cruciferae* which originates from the word "cross," referring to the arrangement of the four flower petals. The showy, yellow petals of this biennial or short-lived perennial are each up to ½ inch long. Its fruits mature into conspicuous, four-angled pods up to 4 inches in length. The stiff, unbranched stems have downy hairs giving it a grayish appearance. The long, narrow leaves tend to curve downward. The herb is widespread in dry or sandy prairie in the central and western states.

1x   Stockert photo

WESTERN SALSIFY

Tragopogon dubius   Composite Family   May – Aug.

A native herb of Europe, the deep taproot of this perennial allows it to compete successfully on dry prairie, waste ground, and roadsides. The pale-yellow flower heads, 2 or more inches across, grow singly at the ends of stems that are 1 to 3 feet tall. With fruiting heads which produce seeds with "parachutes," it is closely related to dandelions (*Taraxacum* sp.). Young plants have been used as potherbs and as greens. The coagulated, milky juice in the stems was considered by Indians to be a remedy for indigestion.

1/2x   Stockert photo

TUMBLEMUSTARD

Sisymbrium altissimum   Mustard Family   May — Sept.

An undesirable herb of fields and waste places,
this winter annual begins its growth in the fall and
eventually obtains a height of 3 feet or more. The
leaves of the irregularly branched plant are
linearly divided. After blooming, many long seed
pods develop. Late in the growing season, the
plant breaks off at ground level and is blown
by the wind, spreading seeds which infest
cultivated areas. Prairie tribes and
early pioneers used the seeds for flavoring foods.
Indians also ground them into meal which was used
in making gruel (a liquid food made by boiling).

2x   Stockert photo

STEMLESS HYMENOXYS

Hymenoxys acaulis   Composite Family   mid May — July

The word *acaulis*, meaning "stemless," refers to
the leafless stalks, or scapes, which bear the flower
heads. These blossoms are slightly over 2 inches in
diameter. The yellow, ray florets have three prominent
"teeth" at their ends. The leaves of this prairie
perennial are lance-shaped or oblong, and grow in a
cluster at soil level. Plants are usually less than
a foot tall. Although rare in North Dakota, the herb
is frequently seen in dry places in other areas of
the plains states.

1/3x   Stockert photo

COMMON MARSH-MARIGOLD

Caltha palustris   Buttercup Family   late May — June

The name "Marigold" is a misnomer in this case
because it is more appropriately applied to members
of the Composite Family. Not widely common
throughout the northern plains, this perennial herb is,
however, abundant in marshes and at the bases of
seepage slopes in the eastern Dakotas. The flowers, up
to 2 inches across, are strikingly waxy yellow. Lacking
petals, the showy structures are actually sepals.
The Dakota Sioux ate the new spring growth as
greens. When boiled, it served as a potherb.

1/2x   Van Bruggen photo

PRAIRIE GROUNDSEL

Senecio plattensis   Composite Family   late May – June

Of the more than 20 kinds of groundsel, or ragwort as they are sometimes called, this is one of the most common in the prairie. The vegetation of this perennial herb has a cottony layer of hairs on its surface. Up to 10 flower heads cluster at the top of stems which grow to about 18 inches tall. A toxin produced by some groundsels causes liver damage and is called stomach staggers in grazing animals. The various groundsels are hard to tell apart because of their similarity in appearance.

1x   Stockert photo

MISSOURI PINCUSHION

Neomamillaria missouriensis   Cactus Family   late May – June

The light yellow flowers of this almost spherical cactus betray its presence, for when not in flower, it is difficult to find among prairie grasses as only the upper portion protrudes above the prairie turf. The succulent stem, about 1 to 3 inches in diameter, is densely covered with spines. The small, rounded fruits are green until the following spring when they mature and turn scarlet. They nestle within the spines resembling eggs in a nest, hence another common name, Birds Nest Cactus Usually growing in clusters of two to six, it is frequently found in dry prairies.

1/2x   Stockert photo

STIFFSTEM FLAX

Linum rigidum   Flax Family   late May – Aug.

The flowers of this prairie native open in the early forenoon but wither and fall off when the sun becomes hot. The herbs are annual and have slender, branched stems about 1 foot tall. The leaves are long and narrow. Seeds are formed in small, hard capsules that are yellow and split when mature. Several native flax species have been responsible for livestock poisoning. The poison is a cyanide compound that interferes with cellular respiration.

3x   Stockert photo

YELLOW LADY SLIPPER

Cypripedium calceolus   Orchid Family   June

This well-known orchid is wide spread
in North America as well as in Asia and Europe.
In our area it is fairly common in rich woods
of the Black Hills. The single stemed plant
grows up to 2 feet tall with several broad
leaves. Usually one, but sometimes two striking
yellow flowers last for several weeks.
The slipper, or lip, is up to 2 inches long.
The lateral petals are spirally twisted and may
be brown or greenish-yellow. Enjoy this orchid
where it is found because it cannot be
transplanted successfully.

1/2x   Van Bruggen photo

YELLOW BOG ORCHID

Habernaria hyperborea   Orchid Family   June — July

Some of the orchids are not as showy
as others. This one has small yellow-green
flowers less than one inch long arranged in
a tight spike about 6 inches long. The lip
is less than ½ inch in length. In the northern
plains this orchid is usually less than 2 feet
tall. It grows in low, moist places in woods
of the Black Hills and meadows elsewhere
in the region. Often times it occurs in
dense stands but is not noticed because of
the small inconspicuous flowers and small
stature.

2/3x   Van Bruggen photo

YELLOW PAINTED-CUP

Castilleja sulphurea   Snapdragon Family   June — July

The leafy bracts beneath the tight spike
of flowers on the Yellow Painted-Cup remain
for many weeks after the flowers mature.
Typical of the painted-cups, the small,
irregularly shaped flowers are highly adapted
for insect pollination. A perennial herb,
this one grows from a woody base. Stems are
about 18 inches tall with many lance-shaped
leaves. It is particularly common in meadows
and open wooded hillsides of the Black Hills
but is uncommon elsewhere.

2/3x   Van Bruggen photo

PALE MOUNTAIN-DANDELION
Agoseris glauca   Composite Family   June – July

The flower heads of this perennial bloom before the
prairie grasses grow tall enough to obscure them. As
in Common Dandelion (see page 7), all of
the sometimes reddish blossoms are really many
strap-like ray florets which form heads at the ends
of leafless stems. The plant has milky juice in the
stems. Its narrow, waxy-whitened leaves grow in a
crowded rosette at the base of the herb. It sends
a slender taproot deep and grows in moist areas of
prairie swales, occurring more commonly westward.

1x   Van Bruggen photo

DESERT PRINCESPLUME
Stanleya pinnata   Mustard Family   June – July

Bright yellow, stalked flowers and drooping pods on
3-foot, waxy stems make this sometimes-woody-based
herb, or subshrub, a conspicuous sentinel of dry
prairie knolls. The flowering plumes form as a result
of continued growth of the stem tips. The stems bear
symmetrically-lobed leaves which are common of many
members of the Mustard Family. This perennial is
well-known by ranchers as an indicator of soils
containing selenium, a poisonous element which is
easily absorbed by some plants. Although the
plant accumulates selenium, animals do
not eat enough to be poisoned.

1/6x   Kravig photo

SILKTOP DALEA
Dalea aurea   Legume Family   June – July

The blossoms of this perennial open from the base
to the top of the dense spike over a 4 to 6 week
period. Each spike is up to 3 inches long and over
½ inch wide. The leaves, typical of the Legume
Family, are made up of many, small, egg-shaped
leaflets. Plains Indians crushed the leaves to
prepare a drink for relieving colic and dysentery.
Also called Silktop Indigobush, it has a woody base
and grows on dry slopes and hillsides. Though often
seen in the north central plains, it has not been
reported from North Dakota.

1x   Van Bruggen photo

WATER HYSSOP

Bacopa rotundifolia   Snapdragon Family   July

The leaves of the Water Hyssop are character-
istically rounded in outline and without stalks.
Plants are rooted in the mud of shallow
water with the stems floating to the surface.
Flowers are yellow to white, with petals
about ½ inch long. They extend several
inches above the water level and are easily
seen. This plant occurs throughout the
northern plains in springs and ponds. It
is spread by migrating waterfowl that eat
or otherwise carry seeds from one place to
another. Other species of Water Hyssop are
common in the tropics.

1x   Van Bruggen photo

TICKSEED

Coreopsis palmata   Composite Family   July

A native of the true prairie in the eastern
part of the Great Plains, this tickseed
has narrow, three-parted leaves that are
scattered on the stems. At flowering time
the plants may be 2 to 3 feet tall. This
plant gets its common name from the fact
that the seed-like fruits or achenes are
"bug-like", which is the meaning of the
Greek word *Coreopsis.*

1/3x   Van Bruggen photo

BRACTED UMBRELLA PLANT

Eriogonum flavum   Buckwheat Family   July — Aug.

The many small, yellow flowers in a tight
umbel and the leafy bracts immediately below
make this prairie native attractive and easily
recognized. It has a woody taproot that
grows down to 8 or more feet below the soil
surface. Eroded clay bluffs and exposed
knolls are favorite habitats for this plant.
There are over 20 species of umbrella plant
in the Great Plains and they are commonly
encountered in the western part of the
northern plains. North American Indians
collected the roots as a winter survival
food.

1/3x   Van Bruggen photo

15

MATCHBRUSH
Gutierrezia sarethrae   Composite Family   July – Aug.

The thin, yellow to brown bases of this
shrub that become woody give this common
prairie native the name Matchbrush. Much
branched, it grows to 2 or more feet tall on
dry hillsides throughout the Great Plains.
The leaves are narrow and have small, resinous
dots. Individual flower heads are less than
¼ inch across. In winter Matchbrush serves
as browse for mammals that live on the
plains. Indians also used the plants for brooms,
fuel, and thatching.

3/4x   Van Bruggen photo

YELLOW MONKEY FLOWER
Mimulus guttatus   Snapdragon Family   July – Aug.

Swampy areas, potholes of the prairie,
and springy areas in the western plains
often have Yellow Monkey Flowers growing at
their margins. Rooted in the mud, the stems
extend above the water level or grow in
patches adjacent to the water. The leaves
are rounded, toothed, and without stalks.
Yellow flowers up to an inch in length, with
a prominent, bearded area in the throat, top
the stem. The term monkey flower refers to
the "face-like" appearance of the flower.

3/4x   Van Bruggen photo

FIVE-NERVED HELIANTHELLA
Helianthella quinquenervis   Composite Family   July – Aug.

Two characteristics distinguish this tall,
yellow-flowered perennial. The long, stalked
flower head is nodded to the side and the
principal leaves are prominently five-nerved.
The name *Helianthella* means "sunflower
like." However, the central disk of flowers
on the head is yellow and not brown as in
the Common Sunflower. Five-nerved Helianthella
is a native of the mountainous regions west
of the plains and is also found along streams
in meadows of the Black Hills.

1/6x   Van Bruggen photo

BUTTER-AND-EGGS

Linaria vulgaris   Snapdragon Family   June — Sept.

This perennial owes its common name to the color of its blossoms. The flower structure is similar to that of the garden snapdragons and, like them, is highly adapted for insect pollination. One of the petals is modified, forming a long, downward projecting spur which contains a nectary. Unbranched stems grow up to 1 or 2 feet from a dense root system. The narrow leaves are numerous. Introduced from Europe, it is now widely established as a roadside herb. It commonly escapes from garden cultivation and forms large patches several yards in diameter.

1x   Van Bruggen photo

UPRIGHT PRAIRIE-CONEFLOWER

Ratibida columnifera   Composite Family   June — Sept.

A perennial with a spreading root system, this herb grows to 3 feet tall. The few, linearly dissected leaves are covered with a dense layer of hairs. "Coneflower" refers to the column, or cone, of tiny tubular flowers in the center of the flower head. At maturity these become single-seeded fruits, called achenes, which are similar to sunflower seeds. Prairie Indians gathered the heads during flowering time and made a tea-like beverage from them. Common in the Central States, the plant is one of our dominant prairie species.

1x   Stockert photo

LEAFY SPURGE

Euphorbia podperae   Spurge Family   June — Sept.

Leafy Spurge has been known as a toxic plant for several hundred years. A native of Eurasia, it has become naturalized in most of North America east of the Rockies. The herb is common on roadsides, in fields, and in other disturbed areas. Several states list this perennial as one of their 10 most noxious weeds. Growing in large, dense patches from a deep, bulb-like root, or rhizome system, it is difficult to eradicate. The prominent, yellowish parts are leafy bracts which are located just below the non-showy flowers.

1/3x   Van Bruggen photo

BUFFALOBUR
Solanum rostratum Nightshade Family June – Oct.

Buffalobur inhabits overgrazed pastures which have
some nitrate reserves. An annual herb, it grows 1 to
2 feet tall. Its leaves are deeply divided with
rounded lobes and look like those of the garden
watermelon. The flowers resemble tomato or potato
blossoms. Spiny capsules develop after flowering
and hold many, small, black seeds. These are
sporadically distributed when the plant breaks off
at ground level, a common occurrence late in the
growing season. Numerous spines which cover the
vegetation discourage grazing animals. Several
closely related species, including Black Nightshade
(*S. nigrum*), are very poisonous.

1x Stockert photo

PRAIRIE DOGWEED
Dyssodia papposa Composite Family June – Oct.

Sandy areas, roadsides, and prairie dog towns are
common habitats for this ill-smelling annual. It is
frequent throughout South Dakota, Nebraska, and to
the west and east of these states. The herb produces
many, small, hard, non-splitting fruits, each with
one seed. Leaves are deeply cut into long, narrow,
compound segments. The bitter odor emitted from
small, yellow glands that dot the vegetation
irritates the nose. Plains Indians snuffed the
pulverized leaves and tops to cause nosebleeds
which supposedly relieved headaches. The
low and much branched plants are avoided by
grazing animals.

5x Stockert photo

CURLYCUP GUMWEED
Grindelia squarrosa Composite Family June – Nov.

This much-branched biennial invades disturbed areas
in the plains. Both the leaves and the curved bracts
of the yellow flower heads exude a sticky material
from minute glands. After flowering, tiny seeds
mature, each with an awn, or protruding bristle,
which aids in distribution by the wind. Dakota
Indians prepared a decoction of the plant for
treating children with colic. Other plains tribes
extracted the gummy material for use against
asthma and bronchitis. Early pioneers used the
herb as a treatment for whooping cough and as an
ingredient for asthma cigarettes.

1x Stockert photo

COMMON PRICKLYPEAR

Opuntia polycantha   Cactus Family   mid June – July

The term "pricklypear" is generally used
for cacti that have flat, jointed stems. Leaves are
very short-lived. They drop off soon after the
formation of a new portion of the stem which takes
over the functions of the leaves. The thick stem
also serves as a succulent, water storage organ. The
blossoms of this perennial are large, waxy, and
usually yellow with reddish centers. When in bloom,
the pricklypears are a mass of yellow on dry buttes
or mesas. The red, pulpy fruits of this species are
edible and tasty. Early settlers made jellies and
jams from them.

1/2x   Stockert photo

COMMON SUNFLOWER

Helianthus annuus   Composite Family   late June – Oct.

Although it is the state flower of Kansas, this
annual is found from the East Coast to the foothills
of the Rocky Mountains. The herbs vary in height
from 1 to 10 feet and bear flower heads that are 2
to 6 inches in diameter. Several varieties are
cultivated for their seeds which when roasted are
eaten like peanuts. Historically, the seeds served
as a favorite food of the Plains Indians who roasted
and ground them for bread and gruel, or extracted
the oils for use in cooking.

1/2x   Van Bruggen photo

FRINGED LOOSESTRIFE

Lysimachia ciliata   Primrose Family   July – Aug.

The deep yellow, five-parted flowers of this perennial
typify the loosestrifes. Short hairs edge the petals and
leafstalks. The petals last only a few days. After they
fall, berries develop, each containing several angular
seeds. Stems grow 1 to 3 feet tall bearing broad leaves
that are opposite. The herb is found in thickets, rich
woods, shores, and other moist areas of the eastern
plains and further eastward.

1x   Van Bruggen photo

GRAYHEAD PRAIRIE-CONEFLOWER
Ratibida pinnata Composite Family July — Aug.

A tall and erect perennial, this prairie-coneflower commonly grows up to 4 feet or more. It is usually branched in the upper half. The center of the flower head, the disk, is dome-like. The outer 10 to 12, petal-like ray florets droop almost as soon as they develop fully. The large leaves are pinnately divided which means the leaflets are on each side of a common stem. It is a showy, midsummer herb of roadsides and edges of thickets in the Dakotas and Nebraska and eastward.

1/4x Van Bruggen photo

COMPASS-PLANT
Silphium laciniatum Composite Family July — Aug.

Sunlight causes the large, irregularly lobed leaves at the base of this perennial to grow with their edges running generally in a north-south direction. Each leaf is up to a foot long and 6 inches wide. The yellow flower heads grow right from the stout stem which may be as high as 4 to 6 feet. Because the juice in the stem is resinous, the plant is also called Rosinweed. Prairie Indians chewed the thick, juicy stem which at first tastes bitter but becomes tolerable after some chewing. This herb prefers the prairies of the eastern plains.

1/4x Van Bruggen photo

CUP ROSINWEED
Silphium perfoliatum Composite Family July — Aug.

Two characteristics identify this coarse perennial. First, the fused bases of the opposite main leaves form cups around the stem, and second, the stem is angular and almost square. These herbs reach 6 feet tall or more with several branches at the top, each with two to four flower heads which are nearly 3 inches in diameter. The plant is frequently found in moist, open places and in roadside ditches of the eastern part of the Great Plains.

1/4x Van Bruggen photo

FLOWER-OF-AN-HOUR

Hibiscus trionum   Mallow Family   July – Aug.

The genus *Hibiscus* has many striking flowers,
both wild and cultivated. Most are native to the
tropics, especially Hawaii. All have flaring,
colorful petals around a central column which is
filled with pollen sacs and topped by the pollen
receiving surface, the stigma. Flowers of this
species open for only a few hours each morning.
The leaves are deeply cut into three parts. The herb
grows to less than 2 feet tall. A native of Europe,
Flower-of-an-hour is now a common annual of fields
and abandoned cultivated areas in the eastern plains.

2/3x   Van Bruggen photo

BLACKEYED-SUSAN

Rudbeckia hirta   Composite Family   July – Aug.

Many Midwest meadows in August are literally
yellow with the flowers of this biennial or short-
lived perennial. Widespread in the United States,
the herb grows well in disturbed ground and on
roadsides. Plants have harsh hairs on their surfaces.
Stems are 1 to 2 feet tall. The 2½-inch flower heads
have petal-like, yellowish-orange ray florets which
bleach somewhat toward maturity. Several forms of
Rudbeckia have been adapted for cultivation
and are called Golden Glow.

1x   Van Bruggen photo

COMMON EVENING-PRIMROSE

Oenothera biennis   Evening-primrose Family   July – Sept.

The four yellow petals of this biennial herb are
attached to the top of the ovary. Flowers are
arranged in a spike-like fashion on stems which may
grow up to 5 feet tall. Late in the season there
may be over 50 oval fruits clustered along the
upper 18 inches of the stem. These pods release
their many seeds over a considerable period of time.
Inhabiting waste places and roadsides, it grows in
most of temperate North America and Canada.

1x   Stockert photo

ROUGH OX-EYE
Heliopsis helianthoides   Composite Family   July – Sept.

This perennial with its paired, opposite leaves
and smooth stem reaching up 2 to 5 feet looks very
much like a sunflower. The term *helianthoides* means
"sunflower-like." Blooming individually for a
considerable time, the 2 - to 3-inch flower heads have
a center disk of small florets which is conical.
This feature along with its opposite leaves
distinguishes this herb from the sunflowers. Rough
Ox-eye is common in prairie remnants along roads and
at the edges of thickets in the northern plains.

1/4x   Van Bruggen photo

TENPETAL BLAZINGSTAR
Mentzelia decapetala   Loasa Family   July – Sept.

Occurring on dry hillsides and eroded clay banks of
the northern plains, this biennial has stout stems
and deep roots. The herbs grow up to 2 feet, with
harshly toothed leaves up to 8 inches long. The
yellowish, cream-colored flowers open in the evening
and are pollinated by night-flying insects, primarily
moths. Its flower structure is similar to that of cactus.
The fruit is a pod up to 2 inches long, containing
many flattened seeds. Prairie Indians squeezed the
juice from the stems for treatment of fevers.

1/2x   Stockert photo

MISSOURI GOLDENROD
Solidago missouriensis   Composite Family   July – Sept.

This perennial herb is probably the most common
goldenrod in the northern plains. The brown to green
stems have a polished appearance and rise from
creeping, underground roots. Narrow leaves crowd
the stem. The flower heads grow on ends of branches
that curve out and down from the main stem.
Reaching a height of 8 to 30 inches, this early
blooming goldenrod grows in a variety of habitats
including dry prairie and other open places.

1/2x   Van Bruggen photo

JERUSALEM ARTICHOKE

Helianthus tuberosus   Composite Family   July — Aug.

The term Jerusalem in the common name of
this sunflower is erroneous and is a corruption
of the Italian word *girasole* meaning
turning to the sun. The word artichoke,
however, is quite appropriate. The roots
of this plant have enlarged, tuberous regions
that are rich in starches and quite edible.
This wildflower is native to the entire
central part of North America and was cultivated
by Indian tribes long before Europeans
came to this continent. It grows in low
meadows and other moist places. The stems
reach 5 feet and are topped by bright
yellow heads.

1/5x   Van Bruggen photo

OWL'S CLOVER

Orthocarpus luteus   Snapdragon Family   July — Aug.

This member of the snapdragon family is
an annual plant which grows in sandy prairie
over the western plains. The common name
refers to the upright or owl-like nature of
the fruits. The small, two-liped flowers are
about ½ inch long and arranged in dense
spikes. Stems are erect and reach 12 inches
or more in height. Its leaves are narrow and
pressed close to the stem. Many hundreds of
small seeds are produced by each plant,
insuring the growth of new plants the
following year.

1/2x   Van Bruggen photo

STIFF GOLDENROD

Solidago rigida   Composite Family   August

The prairie in August is "at attention"
with the erect and rigid stems of this
perennial goldenrod. The stems are stout,
unbranched, and up to 3 feet tall. It is
also distinguished by the dense, crown-like
cluster of flowers topping the stem. The
thick, woody roots are branched and grow
deeply into the prairie turf. Stiff Goldenrod
inhabits upland prairies from Minnesota to
Texas and west to the Rocky Mountains.

1/4x   Van Bruggen photo

COMMON MULLEIN

Verbascum thapsus   Snapdragon Family   July — Sept.

Native of Europe, this plant was brought by man
to many of the places he has disturbed. A biennial,
it produces a basal rosette of large, thick leaves
the first year and an erect, thick stem up to 6 feet
tall the second year. The yellow flowers are up to 1
inch wide and form a long, dense spike at the top
of the fleshy stem. Dead stems may stand erect
for several years after flowering. A familiar herb
of rocky soil, hillsides, and over-grazed pastures,
it is thoroughly established in this region.

1/2x   Van Bruggen photo

PUNCTURE-VINE

Tribulus terrestris   Caltrop Family   July — Oct.

The small flowers of this annual are open only in
the morning. The fruits, or "stickers," are
distinctive because each of their five parts has two
heavy, sharp, ½-inch spines that easily puncture
bicycle tires. The flat vine forms a mat the size of
a square yard or larger. It grows on sandy or thin
soil, and is abundant on railroad ballasts and
roadsides. A native of Europe, this herb now
extends from Eastern United States to the western
edge of the high plains and the southwestern states.

2x   Stockert photo

IRONPLANT GOLDENWEED

Haplopappus spinulosus   Composite Family   July — Oct.

There are over 25 species of goldenweed in the
Great Plains; all are characterized by dense clusters
of yellow flowers at the ends of tough, wiry stems.
This species has compound leaves whose long segments
are spine-tipped, hence the term *spinulosus.* As a
result, grazing animals avoid the plant. A hardy
perennial, it grows in dry prairie from a woody
base and deep root system.

1x   Stockert photo

MAXIMILIAN SUNFLOWER

Helianthus maximiliana Composite Family late July — Sept.

This tall, many-flowered perennial with flexible
stems was named after the German prince, Maximilian,
who made several botanical explorations in North and
South America during the early 1800's. The herb is
a conspicuous inhabitant of swales and other low
places of the plains, where it is usually associated
with tall, prairie grasses. A good identifying
characteristic is its long, narrow leaves that
fold into a V-shape, curving outward from the
stem. Each flower head is 3 or more inches across.
Prairie Indians collected the short rootstocks for food.

1/3x   Van Bruggen photo

RUBBER RABBITBRUSH

Chrysothamnus nauseosus Composite Family late July — Oct.

The generic name, meaning "golden bush," refers
to the many, small, yellow florets that cluster at
the ends of woody branches. Usually each clump of
stems attains 1 to 3 feet in height. When blooming,
it is the most conspicuous flower in many areas
during September. It is a common inhabitant of dry
slopes and eroding bluffs in the western, arid parts
of the Dakotas and Nebraska, and further west.
Prairie Indians used the shrub for medicines, dyes, and
fuel. It also serves as a winter browse for pronghorn,
deer, and elk.

1/2x   Stockert photo

HAIRY GOLDASTER

Chrysopsis villosa Composite Family late July — Oct.

Although the flower head of this perennial herb
resembles that of the asters, there are several
dissimilarities. The most obvious one is that the
ray florets are yellow unlike the usually white
to purple blossoms of the aster. *Villosa* means
"hairy" which refers to the covering of hairs on
the stem and leaf surfaces. Stems grow 6 inches to 2
feet tall depending on the moisture available. Its
deep rootstocks are an adaptation to dry prairie
habitats. This goldaster is common in the western
plains and Black Hills but rare in the eastern
part of the Dakotas and Nebraska.

1/2x   Stockert photo

SAWTOOTH SUNFLOWER

Helianthus grosseserratus   Composite Family   Aug. – Sept.

One of 16 species of sunflower native to the
northern plains, this coarse perennial inhabits open
bottomlands and ditches along roads. The lance-shaped
leaves of the herb have wide "teeth" along the edges.
The branched stems, varying from 3 to 10 feet tall,
bear flower heads that are 3 or more inches across.
The center disk is yellow and smaller than the
brownish-purple disk of Common Sunflower
(see page 19).

1/4x   Van Bruggen photo

SHOWY PARTRIDGE-PEA

Cassia fasciculata   Legume Family   Aug. – Sept.

A common herb of low, sandy areas along rivers
and streams, this annual ranges from Massachusetts
to Texas. It is frequently seen on sand bars along
the Missouri River. The erect stems grow 1 to 3 feet
high bearing compound leaves, each with eight to 12
pairs of leaflets. The flowers have an irregular
symmetry, meaning that each petal has a somewhat
different shape and orientation than the others.
Seeds are produced in small pods and are forcibly
expelled when mature. Weakly toxic to animals, it
and other closely related species are also cathartic.

1/2x   Van Bruggen photo

ROUGH RATTLESNAKE-ROOT

Prenanthes aspera   Composite Family   Aug. – Sept.

The underground parts of this perennial are very
bitter and were believed effective as a treatment
for snakebites. This is yet another example of the
idea that bad taste indicates medicinal value, which
is not true. Stems are tall, up to 5 feet, with
creamy-yellow flower heads arranged along the upper
part as shown. Large, oval, wide-tipped leaves with
short, stiff, surface hairs grow at the base of the
stem. This herb occasionally inhabits moist
swales in the eastern plains.

1/2x   Van Bruggen photo

SHOWY GOLDENROD

Solidago speciosa   Composite Family·   Aug. — Sept.

Speciosa, meaning "beautiful," is a good description
for this goldenrod. Plants, commonly 1 to 2 feet
tall and solitary, grow from a stout, woody root.
The stiff, erect stems bear many leaves that are
larger toward the base. The flower cluster, or
inflorescence, is a tight, cylindrical mass of
yellow heads, each usually with five large ray
florets. This perennial herb inhabits open thickets
and rocky woods as well as the high plains and
Black Hills.

1/2x   Van Bruggen photo

CANADA GOLDENROD

Solidago canadensis   Composite Family   Aug. — Sept.

Of the more than 25 species of goldenrod native to the
high plains, this book includes only five of the
most common. Although some are quite distinctive,
most are hard to tell apart. The yellow flower heads
of Canada Goldenrod have the characteristic arrangement and shape pictured. The leaves have three
prominent veins and are progressively smaller toward
the top of the herb. The stems and leaves look
grayish-green because of their short surface hairs.
This perennial is common in thickets, in open
fields, and on roadsides.

1/3x   Van Bruggen photo

GRAY GOLDENROD

Solidago nemoralis   Composite Family   Aug. — Sept.

The flower clusters of this drought-resistant goldenrod
are generally arranged along one side of a curved
stem. The herb grows from a thick root stock usually
to a height of less than a foot but may grow as high
as 2 feet. The bottom leaves soon die, leaving a barren
lower stem with short leaves toward the top. This
perennial favors dry places on the high plains. Indians
used the flowering of goldenrod as an indication of
when their corn was beginning to ripen.

1/2x   Van Bruggen photo

AMERICAN PLUM
Prunus americana   Rose Family   April – May

This wild plum is common in draws and thickets throughout the Midwest. The shrub-like trees are 6 to 10 feet tall. Older branches become somewhat spiny. The five-parted white flowers, each up to 1 inch wide, bloom in small clusters on second-year wood. The fruits turn reddish-orange, maturing in August and early September. Indians and early pioneers sought the fruits and ate them fresh, dried in the winter, or cooked as a sauce. Wild plum jam is unsurpassed on breakfast toast!

1/2x   Van Bruggen photo

White Flowers

SNOW TRILLIUM
Trillium nivale   Lily Family   April

This photograph was taken in the second week of April where large snow banks on the northern slope of a ravine were melting. In three out of 12 years in this ravine, Snow Trillium was in bloom before the snow had disappeared. Only 3 or 4 inches tall, the herb has three leaves that radiate from the stem at one point and a single white flower at the top of the stem. A native of rich, loamy woods, this perennial reaches the eastern parts of the Dakotas and Nebraska, where the eastern deciduous woods give way to the prairies.

1/3x   Van Bruggen photo

COMMON CHOKECHERRY
Prunus virginiana   Rose Family   April – May

This shrub may grow up to 20 feet or more and is often found in ravines and valleys. The fruits ripen in late July or early August to a dark purple, each one very tart with a single stone. Plains Indians dried the fruits for winter use and ground them up to make into cakes in the summer. They ground both fresh and dried fruits and mixed them with dried meat to make a popular food known as pemmican. Chokecherries make delicious jelly and jam.

1/4x   Stockert photo

CANADA VIOLET

Viola canadensis   Violet Family   April – May

A native of Canada and northern United States, this
perennial herb forms dense stands in shaded woods.
Stems, up to 1 foot tall, bear broad, oval leaves
with irregular teeth. The white flowers have pale
lavender veins or outer edges and may turn purple
as they age. Many seeds are produced that germinate
easily in gardens. Indians ate the young leaves and
stems as greens and also made a beverage of the flowers.

1/2x   Van Bruggen photo

DUTCHMANS-BREECHES

Dicentra cucullaria   Poppy Family   April – June

The soft, green, deeply-cut leaves and the arching
stems of two to eight nodding, white flowers provide
for easy identification of Dutchmans-breeches. An
early spring herb of loamy slopes in eastern timber,
it is found occasionally in the woods of the eastern
part of the Dakotas and Nebraska where prairie
gradually becomes the dominant vegetation. This
perennial grows up to 8 inches from grain-like
tubers. The outer petals of each flower resemble
two inverted sacs. The green fruits are shaped like,
but smaller than, the pods of the garden green pea.

1/2x   Van Bruggen photo

TUFTED EVENING-PRIMROSE

Oenothera caespitosa   Evening-primrose Family   April – Aug.

Also known as Gumbo-lily, this hardy perennial of
dry buttes and clay banks has large white flowers
produced at ground level which turn pink and wilt
in less than a day. This showy evening-primrose is
frequently cultivated as an ornamental. Its fruiting
pods, when mature, are up to 1 inch long. The
principal leaves at the base of the stem are
coarsely toothed. Prairie Indians cooked the stout
taproots of this herb for food. They also prepared a
decoction, a liquid preparation made by boiling,
from the taproots for a treatment against coughs
and other respiratory infections.

1/3x   Stockert photo

RED PUSSYTOES
Antennaria rosea   Composite Family   May — June

Many of the pussytoes are dioecious, that
is, the male plants and female plants grow
separately. This is a photograph of a
female plant. The leaf-like bracts surrounding
the flower heads are tinged with pink. All
of the pussytoes of the northern plains are
perennials. They grow in large mats,
spreading by runners. The leaves of this one
are small and spoon-shaped, with a dense,
white layer of hairs on both surfaces. The
flowering stalks are about 5 inches tall with
white and pink flower parts that are soft
like the toes of a young kitten.

1x   Van Bruggen photo

WATERLEAF
Hydrophyllum virginianum   Waterleaf Family   May — June

The common name of this woodland herb
refers to the watery juice in the stems and
leaves. The stems elongate rapidly in the
spring and begin flowering before the
overhead trees are fully in leaf. The flower
clusters are dense and unroll as the individual
flowers open. Their color may vary from white
to pale lavender. Waterleaf grows in the eastern
parts of the Dakotas and Nebraska where the
woodlands meet the prairie. It is common in
the central and eastern parts of the
United States.

1/3x   Van Bruggen photo

BLOODROOT
Sanguinaria canadensis   Poppy Family   April — May

Poppies the world over have colored or milky
juice in various parts of the plant body.
The Bloodroot is not exception. Its underground stems or rhizomes yield a blood-red
juice when broken. Native American Indians
used it as a dye. They named these dye
producing plants Puccoons (see page 8).
The dainty, white flowers have eight petals.
The supporting flower stalks are naked and
grow to a height of 8 inches in early spring.
Later the leaves expand on stalks that grow
directly from the underground stem. Bloodroot
occurs in rich woods of eastern North and South
Dakota but is rare in the Black Hills.

1/4x   Van Bruggen photo

HOOD PHLOX

Phlox hoodii   Phlox Family   mid April – June

A low perennial with a dense, mat-like appearance,
this herb is a showy plant on prairie knolls and
exposed areas when in bloom. Resistant to drought
because of a deep root system, it prefers dry and
eroded areas where other plants cannot grow. The
grayish leaves are pointed and up to ½ inch long.
The flowers are white to light pink, or sometimes
darker pink, and are relished by sheep. Common in the
high plains, it is rare or absent in eastern North
and South Dakota. Several native species of phlox are
sold commercially for ornamental planting.

1x   Stockert photo

SHADBLOW SERVICEBERRY

Amelanchier humilis   Rose Family   late April

Experts cannot agree on how to classify the eight or
more North American serviceberries into proper
species. This one, a small, shrubby tree that
reaches 10 feet tall, grows in clumps or thickets
on hillsides and on the edges of wooded ravines.
The oval leaves appear after the plant flowers.
Many birds and mammals eat the fruit clusters which
taste remotely like apples but are mealy and dry.
Indians used the twigs and bark for basketry
and weaving.

1/3x   Van Bruggen photo

COMMON STARLILY

Leucocrinum montanum   Lily Family   late April – June

This stemless perennial of plains and hillsides
grows from several fleshy roots that are like coarse
strings radiating out in several directions. All of
the leaves are narrow and grasslike and arise from
a short crown into a rosette. The word *Leucocrinum*
comes from the Greek meaning "white lily." It refers
to the white, star-shaped flowers that open at soil
level. The fruiting capsule, about ½ inch long, forms
just underground. The seeds of this herb will germinate
successfully in cultivation.

1x   Stockert photo

DOWNY PAINTBRUSH
Castilleja sessiliflora   Snapdragon Family   late April – June

These early flowers are long and narrow and are
highly adapted for insect pollination. The petals,
varying from green to yellow, are almost hidden from
view by conspicuous whitish-yellow, leafy bracts. A
perennial herb, it is usually less than 1 foot tall
and grows in clumps on dry prairie, ranging from
Saskatchewan to Texas. Over 100 species occur in the
Rocky Mountains and the Pacific Northwest. Many
are partial root parasites of other plants.

1/2x   Stockert photo

BALLHEAD IPOMOPSIS
Ipomopsis congesta   Phlox Family   late April – June

One of more than 25 species of the Phlox family
native to the western plains and Rocky Mountains,
this densely hairy herb grows from a branched,
woody root system to a height of less than one foot.
White flowers, each ¼ inch wide, thickly cluster or
congest as a rounded head at the top of the plant.
This perennial prefers dry habitats such as the tops
and edges of buttes. It will transplant easily to
gardens. A number of closely related forms called
Gilias are cultivated as ornamentals.

3x   Stockert photo

FLESHY HAWTHORN
Crataegus succulenta   Rose Family   May

This small tree which may grow to more than 10
feet tall has many sharp, unbranched spines on the
branches. The hairy leaves are round with sharp "teeth"
called serrations. Arranged in terminal clusters, the
white, five-petaled flowers are each about ½ inch
across. Small, apple-like fruits mature in August,
each containing three to five nutlets. Plains Indians
ate these fruits after they were pounded into a
meal and baked. Fleshy Hawthorn is frequent in
steep-walled valleys and on the slopes and
tops of ravines.

1/2x   Van Bruggen photo

STARRY SOLOMONPLUME

Smilacina stellata Lily Family May – June

The small, six-petaled, white blossoms of this
perennial form a simple cluster at the top of the
stem. *Stellata*, meaning "star-shaped," refers to
the contour of the flowers. The blooms are followed
by green, black-striped berries that are about ¼
inch thick. Growing from a rooted fibrous rhizome
(thickened underground stem), the 10- to 18-inch
stems are zig-zagged with bright green, lanceolate
leaves. Very common in thickets and woodlands in
temperate North America, this herb is one of our
better known spring flowers.

2x   Stockert photo

TEXTILE ONION

Allium textile Lily Family May – June

Of the many species of wild onion, this is perhaps
the most common on the north central prairie. The
15-inch plants grow from solitary, underground
bulbs which are covered with fibrous, netted veins.
The flower cluster, an umbel (fan-shaped), varies
from white to deep pink. Prairie Indians ate many
kinds of wild onions and prepared decoctions of the
bulb juice for treating sore throats. They also dried
the bulbs for future use as food and flavoring.

1/3x   Stockert photo

GRASSY DEATHCAMAS

Zigadenus venenosus var. *gramineus* Lily Family May – June

Several North American species of deathcamas are
among the most poisonous plants of the plains. An
alkaloid is the toxic substance, producing symptoms
similar to cyanide poisoning. The stems of this
herbaceous perennial grow up to 2 feet from an
onion-like bulb. Flowers are arranged in a loose
spike. Each petal has a half-moon-shaped gland at
its base. The lack of an onion odor distinguishes
deathcamas from the wild onions. However, there
have been cases of poisoning in Indians and
settlers who mistakenly ate them.

2x   Stockert photo

COMMON COMANDRA
Comandra umbellata   Sandalwood Family   May – June

The stems of this perennial arise from an underground
rhizome, or bulb-like root system, which attaches
to the roots of various plants. Technically, it is
called a hemi-parasite, or halfway parasite. Their
roots are never well-developed. The herb does,
however, have the ability to produce its own food
photosynthetically. Clusters of flowers, usually
whitish, develop at the tops of stems that only
reach 4 to 6 inches tall. Widespread in the prairie
where deep turf is available, it is also
found under oak trees.

3x   Stockert photo

WHITE PENSTEMON
Penstemon albidus   Snapdragon Family   May – June

More than 250 species of penstemon, also known as
beardstongue, grow in North America. White Penstemon
often inhabits exposed, dry prairie with calcium-bearing
soil. Several stems about 10 inches high shoot from
a woody root-stock. These stems are covered with
short, soft hairs that are glandular. In contrast to
other prairie penstemons which have various shades
of red to blue flowers, this plant has inch-long,
white blossoms. Their insides are bearded and often
spotted with purple. An herbaceous perennial, this
plant is found mainly in the high plains but does
reach southward to Texas and New Mexico.

1x   Stockert photo

NODDING WHITE TRILLIUM
Trillium cernuum   Lily Family   May – June

Three large leaves nearly hide the single white
flower of this graceful, thin-stemmed herb of rich
woods. *Cernuum*, meaning "nodding" or
"curved downward," is a reference to the drooping
flower that is about 2 inches across with petals
and sepals each numbering three. The 12- to 18-inch
stem grows rapidly from creeping rootstocks. Common
in Eastern United States, this perennial ranges to
the Red River Valley of North Dakota and into
South Dakota and Iowa.

1/2x   Van Bruggen photo

WILD LILY OF THE VALLEY

Maianthemum canadense   Lily Family   May – June

This common wildflower of woodlands, often pine or spruce woods, is found from Labrador to British Columbia and south throughout North America. It is also called the Canada Mayflower. It often is found in dense mats under trees where the stems spread by underground runners. Flower stalks are 3 to 8 inches tall and have two or three, heart-shaped leaves that clasp the stem. Usually members of the lily family have flower parts in threes, but this one has them in twos and fours. In the northern plains it grows in the eastern Dakotas and in the Black Hills.

1/3x   Van Bruggen photo

WHITE LOCOWEED

Oxytropis sericea   Legume Family   June

A close relative of the Lambert Crazyweed, White Locoweed is not as common. It grows in the western and southern parts of the northern plains. As the common name indicates, it possesses a toxic material that can cause poisoning in grazing livestock. The predominant color of the flowers is white but often they are tinged with lavender. The flowering stalks are naked. Leaves are many-parted and arise from soil level as in the other members of the *Oxytropis* group.

1/3x   Van Bruggen photo

PIN CHERRY

Prunus pensylvanica   Rose Family   June – July

The cherries and plums are very much alike when they flower. When they fruit, however, the plums have a groove on one side and a flattened stone. The cherries, on the other hand, have a stone that is smaller and spherical. Pin Cherry has a growth habit that is very similar to the wild plum. The shrubby trees are 6-10 feet tall with flower clusters similarly arranged, however, the flowers of the cherry are smaller. Pin Cherry makes good jam and was used by Indians in making pemmican. It grows in North Dakota and Minnesota and west to the Black Hills in the northern plains.

1/2x   Van Bruggen photo

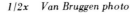

COMMON STRAWBERRY
Fragaria virginiana   Rose Family   May – June

Because of its similarity to cultivated forms,
this wild strawberry needs little description.
Cultivated strawberries were developed by hybrid
crosses from several native stocks. This herb
inhabits open areas and loamy woods from the East
Coast to the Rockies and south to Oklahoma. The
stems are very short and perennial. Most vegetative
reproduction occurs by surface runners. Although it
flowers in relatively large numbers, few fruits are
set and they are much smaller than the cultivated
varieties. Woodland Indians prized the fruits when
available. They also prepared an infusion from the
leaves which they drank as a tea.

1/2x   Van Bruggen photo

BRADBURY CRYPTANTHA
Cryptantha celosioides   Borage Family   May – Sept.

This harsh, bristly biennial of prairie slopes and
ridges has long, stiff hairs covering the stems and
leaves which give it a grayish appearance. The
conspicuous flowers are ½ inch or less in diameter
and are arranged along short branches that become
recurved, or curved downward. Also known as Butte
Candle, this herb is an inhabitant of the western
plains. It is common in the sandhills of Nebraska
but is rare east of the Missouri River in the
Dakotas. Grazing animals avoid it because of the
spiny hairs.

1/4x   Stockert photo

FIELD BINDWEED
Convolvulus arvensis   Morning-glory Family   May – Sept.

Many farmers call this plant Creeping Jenny.
Difficult to eradicate from fields because of deep,
spreading roots, it can be destroyed only by
repeated, heavy doses of weed killer. A native of
Europe, this perennial has become naturalized in most
of the United States and Canada. The pinkish-white
petals are joined to form a funnel-shaped flower,
typical of the Morning-glory Family. The leaves are
somewhat arrow-shaped. Many states have the herb
listed as one of their noxious weeds.

1/2x   Stockert photo

LOW FLEABANE

Erigeron pumilus   Composite Family   mid May – June

The word *pumilus*, meaning "small," refers to the
size of the herb. The stout, deep taproot is
perennial and has the ability to persist in
extremely dry places. Many glandular hairs cover
the long, narrow leaves. Flower heads are
approximately 1 inch in diameter. The ray florets,
usually white, have narrow, strap-shaped petals.
This characteristic, plus the presence of many
leaf-like bracts at the base of the heads, distinguishes
fleabanes from asters. Low Fleabane is commonly
found in plains but not as far east as eastern Nebraska
or the eastern Dakotas.

1/2x   Stockert photo

RACEMED POISONVETCH

Astragalus racemosus   Legume Family   mid May – Aug.

One of several *Astragalus* species poisonous to
livestock, this herb accumulates selenium, which
causes "blind staggers" and alkali disease in
grazing animals. The coarse, erect stems bear
yellowish-white flowers which are attached singly,
each with its own small stalk. The plant
grows in clumps from a stout taproot and reaches
about 2 feet in height. This perennial has a wide
geographic distribution in the northern plains
and is considered to be a selenium indicator of
soils where it is found.

2x   Stockert photo

INLAND CEANOTHUS

Ceanothus herbaceus   Buckthorn Family   late May – June

This close relative of New Jersey Tea (*C. americanus*)
is a bushy shrub which grows up to 2 feet. Preferring
sandy or dry prairie hillsides and thicket edges,
it is frequent in Nebraska and South Dakota,
although it has not been reported in North
Dakota. The small, white blossoms occur in a showy,
dense cluster called a panicle. The leaves are ovate,
or egg-shaped, with fine serrations. Young leaves and
flowering stalks can be dried and steeped, providing
an acceptable substitute for tea. However,
objectionable alkaloids are extracted if
steeped too long.

2/3x   Van Bruggen photo

MOSCHATEL
Adoxa moschatellina   Moschatel Family   June – July

This wildflower is included
here, not because it is common, but because
of its rarity in the northern plains. It
grows on moss-covered rocks in canyons
where it is cool and shaded. Although
it ranges from Ontario west to Utah, in
our area it is found only in the Black
Hills. The common name is derived from
the musky odor of the tuberous roots.
Another common name of the plant is Musk-
root. The plants are very small, not
more than 5 inches tall, and have three to
six, tiny, green-white flowers at the
top of the stem.

2x   Van Bruggen photo

FALSE GROMWELL
Onosmodium molle   Borage Family   June – July

Native prairie remnants usually have
False Gromwell as a frequent inhabitant.
Typical of the borage family, this member
has sticky hairs on the leaves and flowers
in coiled clusters that unroll as they
open. Several stems grow from a deep
seated rootstock. At maturity they may
be as tall as 2 feet. The white to green,
funnel-shaped flowers are about ½ inch
long. False Gromwell is common in the
northern plains, and ranges from
Minnesota to New Mexico.

1/2x   Van Bruggen photo

GREEN GENTIAN
Swertia radiata   Gentian Family   June

There are several green gentians in the
western United States. This one is found
from the Black Hills of South Dakota west
to California. A prominent plant, it has
a stout, unbranched stem that reaches over
3 feet high. The long, sword-shaped leaves
radiate out from the stem in a whorled fashion.
The flowers are white to green with purple
spots, and each petal face has a pair of
glandular areas. It grows in moist areas
of open woods and valleys.

1/5x   Van Bruggen photo

SEGOLILY

Calochortus gunnisonii Lily Family late May — June

The entire plant is edible; however, it was the bulb that provided food for Indians. It was made the state flower of Utah after being credited for saving the lives of Mormon pioneers when their crops were damaged by crickets. The bulbs, about an inch across, taste much like potato when boiled or baked and are quite nutritious. Flowers are creamy-white with a magenta base. The grasslike leaves are few and roll inward. This perennial herb inhabits hillsides and dry, open areas in the western half of the Dakotas and Nebraska and westward. The name "Sego" is of Shoshone origin.

1x   Stockert photo

PALE EVENING-PRIMROSE

Oenothera albicaulis Evening-primrose Family late May — June

There are more than 25 species of evening-primrose that are native to the high plains. This one is a branched annual that grows up to 18 inches tall. Each showy, white flower is up to 4 inches in diameter. They are short-lived, lasting only a day or so. As is typical for cream-colored or white flowers, they open in the evening when their nectaries attract night-flying insects. This herb prefers dry, sandy soil of prairie or sandy washouts of stream beds.

1/2x   Stockert photo

LARGEFLOWER TOWNSENDIA

Townsendia grandiflora Composite Family late May — June

This perennial herb grows sparsely in dry prairie or on eroded clay banks. It is inconspicuous except when in bloom. Large in comparison with the rest of the plant, the flower heads display yellow centers surrounded by pinkish-tinged, white ray florets. The 2-inch heads appear singly or in small clusters from the short stems which branch from a substantial root. Indians ate the branched, root crown of this plant and pioneers used its flowers to decorate churches at Easter time.

1x   Stockert photo

COMMON YARROW
Achillea millefolium   Composite Family   late May – Aug.

Millefolium, meaning "thousand leaves," describes
the many segments of compound leaves which give this
perennial a fern-like appearance before it blooms
in clusters of flower heads. This is a naturalized
plant from Europe where for centuries it has been
used as a medicine. Here it is common in waste
places, overgrazed pastures, and along roadsides.
The herb, especially the leaves, produces an aromatic
volatile oil and was steeped for tea, chewed for
toothache, and generally used as a stimulant or tonic.
Winnebago Indians wadded the leaves in their ears as
a treatment for earaches.

1/2x   Van Bruggen photo

SMOOTH SUMAC
Rhus glabra   Cashew Family   June

A shrubby plant with several stems, Smooth Sumac
prefers open hillsides and the edges of woods. The
greenish-white flowers grow in dense clusters at the
ends of branches. In autumn the leaves turn bright
red before falling. The deep red fruits, which remain
when other food is snow covered, provide a plentiful,
alternate source of winter food for birds. Indians
steeped the fruits for tea and pounded the seeds into
flour which was made into gruel, a bread-like food.
This was not part of their regular diet but served as
survival food during severe winters.

1/3x   Van Bruggen photo

MEADOW ANEMONE
Anemone canadensis   Buttercup Family   June – July

The white sepals on Meadow Anemone look like
petals. As in all the anemones, true petals are lacking.
Spreading by rhizomes, this perennial frequently
inhabits roadside ditches and moist prairie. Hairy
stems grow up to 2 feet with leaves deeply and
irregularly lobed but oval to round in outline.
Small, dry, one-seeded fruits, called achenes,
crowd together forming a bristly, spherical
head. Medicine men of the Plains Indians made a
decoction from the vegetative parts of the herb to
wash the wounds of their people. Although rare
westward, it is common in the eastern Dakotas
and Nebraska, and eastward.

1/3x   Van Bruggen photo

INDIAN HEMP

Apocynum cannabinum   Dogbane Family   June – July

The name Dogbane is derived from a
Greek name whose true meaning is lost and
perhaps has nothing to do with dogs. The
term Indian Hemp does relate to the fact
that Indians collected and processed the
willowy stems to make articles such as mats
and baskets. A perennial, it grows in open
soils and thickets over the plains. The
white flowers top the stems which reach
3 or more feet high. When broken, the
stems yield a milky juice. Indian Hemp is
a relative of the milkweeds but has pods
that are longer and very narrow.

1/3x   Van Bruggen photo

MOUNTAIN BALM

Ceanothus velutinus   Buckthorn Family   June – July

A number of common names have been applied
to this member of the *Ceanothus* group
but Mountain Balm is perhaps the most used.
A large shrub, it is found at middle
altitudes in the Rocky Mountains and at
upper altitudes in the Black Hills. The
leaves are thick and evergreen, that is,
do not drop off in the fall. They serve
as valuable winter browse for deer and
elk. The white flowers are produced in dense,
upright clusters. Note the similarity to
Inland Ceanothus (see page 37). Many small
ovoid fruits are formed after flowering.

1/2x   Van Bruggen photo

PALE DOGWOOD

Cornus amomum   Dogwood Family   June – July

This shrub is not the most common member
of the dogwood family in the central and
northern plains. That distinction belongs
to the closely related species, Red Osier,
which has flowers and leaves very similar
to the one illustrated, but possesses
prominently reddish branches. The shrubby
dogwoods are densely branched and reach 10
feet tall. They are important as understory
shrubs in woodlands and are common along
waterways. Their fruits are berry-like and
provide valuable winter feed for wildlife.

3/4x   Van Bruggen photo

PLAINS LARKSPUR
Delphinium virescens   Buttercup Family   June – July

The native habitat for this prairie perennial extends westward from Iowa to the foothills of the Rocky Mountains. The dissected, crowfoot-like leaves contain an alkaloid called delphinine, which is poisonous to grazing animals. The flowers, up to 1½ inches long, are arranged along the main stem. They are adapted for receiving night-flying moths who act as pollinators. One sepal of the flower has a modified base forming an upward projecting spur which contains nectar. When in bloom, the herbs are conspicuous in dry areas of the high plains where they may grow to more than 30 inches tall.

1x   Van Bruggen photo

SCARLET ELDERBERRY
Sambucus pubens   Honeysuckle Family   June – July

These large shrubs, 5 to 10 feet tall, usually grow in thickets and are particularly noticeable in the Black Hills. Small, white flowers form branched, dense clusters called cymes. Each cyme is 2 to 8 inches across. The profuse, red to purple berries ripen in July and August and are bitter to the taste because of the presence of saponin, a soapy-like material. Wildlife carefully avoid eating them. A closely related species, the American, or Common, Elderberry (*S. canadensis*), is frequent eastward. Its berries are a deeper purple and are edible.

1/2x   Kravig photo

OX-EYE DAISY
Chrysanthemum leucanthemum   Composite Family   June – Aug.

This herb is a native of Eurasia and has become naturalized throughout most of temperate North America. It is frequently seen along roadsides, in disturbed prairie, and on railroad embankments. A perennial, it spreads underground by a rhizome, an elongated bulb-like root system. Stems grow up to 2 feet with solitary flower heads. The outer, white ray florets account for the name *leucanthemum* which means "white flower." Ox-eye Daisy transplants to gardens very successfully; in fact, it may take over a garden!

2/3x   Van Bruggen photo

BLUESTEM PRICKLYPOPPY

Argemone polyanthemos   Poppy Family   June – Sept.

Large flowers up to 4 inches across characterize
this more or less prickly plant. The blossoms, each
with six papery petals, are followed by spiny-edged
fruits that are about an inch long. Its leaves are
silvery blue and also have a spiny edge. A sticky,
yellow juice oozes out when the stems are broken.
Animals carefully avoid this annual herb because
of its spines and unpalatable juices. The plant
grows up to 3 feet or more and is particularly
common in the sandhills of Nebraska although
it is seen in other parts of that state and in
South Dakota.

1x   Stockert photo

CATNIP

Nepeta cataria   Mint Family   June – Sept.

This flower is an excellent example of
specialization for insect pollination. Each blossom
is about ½ inch long, with an open throat that
welcomes each insect visitor. The flowers are arranged
in spikes at the ends of branched stems that grow 2
to 4 feet tall. The arrow-shaped leaves with rounded
"teeth" are softly hairy and aromatic. The minty
aroma of the herb does attract cats who enjoy
rolling in it. Old manuals of medicine recommended
extracts of Catnip for curing colic in infants. A
native of Europe, Catnip has become a perennial
resident throughout the United States.

3/4x   Van Bruggen photo

WESTERN SNOWBERRY

Symphoricarpos occidentalis   Honeysuckle Family   mid June – Aug.

The white fruits of this shrub are easier to see
than the white to pink flowers which bloom in dense
clusters. Two-foot-tall Western Snowberry favors
open hillsides and replaces prairie grasses that are
overgrazed by livestock. Dakota Indians used the
stems and roots as a survival food and the fruits
as a laxative. They also pounded the roots and steeped
them to make a medicine for treating colds. Small
amounts of saponin-like alkaloids are present
in the leaves.

3x   Stockert photo

SPIKENARD
Aralia recemosa   Ginseng Family   July

This member of the ginseng family has
many white flowers in several tight umbels
and is distinguished by the large, divided
leaves. The stems are irregularly branched
and commonly grow to heights of 3 feet or
more. The roots are aromatic and may have
been used for ointments. A closely related
species, *Aralia nudicaulis*, also found
in our area, has aromatic roots which can
be used as a substitute for sarsaparilla.
Spikenard grows in woods in the eastern
parts of the northern plains and south to
Georgia and Mexico.

1/4x   Van Bruggen photo

BRACTED ORCHID
Habenaria viridis   Orchid Family   June – July

This orchid is quite common and is easily
recognized by the long, green bracts beneath
the flowers. Unlike most orchids it is not
very showy. The flowers are mostly green with
some white color on the lips. The lip has
two or three teeth or indentations, a
distinguishing characteristic not found on
the Yellow Bog Orchid (see page 13). Stems
are unbranched and up to 2 feet tall, with
several ovate to lance-shaped leaves. The
Bracted Orchid grows in damp woods throughout the northern plains, including the Black
Hills. There are ten species of *Habenaria*
orchids in this region.

2/3x   Van Bruggen photo

HIGHBUSH CRANBERRY
Viburnum opulus   Honeysuckle Family   June – July

A native of moist woods in the northern
part of the United States and into Canada,
Highbush Cranberry is a woody shrub that
often reaches 6 feet or more. The dark
green leaves have three prominent lobes.
Flowers are in rounded or flat topped in-
in florescences called cymes. Often the
marginal flowers are sterile with large petals.
The small, red fruits are similar to cran-
berries. A number of the *Viburnum* species
are cultivated and commonly called Snowball
Shrubs. In our region Highbush Cranberry
ranges from eastern North Dakota to the
Black Hills.

1/2x   Van Bruggen photo

WHITE PRAIRIECLOVER

Petalostemum candidum   Legume Family   mid June — Sept.

This legume is important for its forage value to
grazing animals. It has small flowers arranged in a
dense spike up to 2 inches long. Flowering starts
at the base and moves up to the tip. Plants are
perennial from woody roots. Stems branch primarily
from the base and grow to a height of 2 feet or
more. The compound leaves are divided into narrow,
linear leaflets. Indian women collected many plants
which they tied together to make crude brooms for
sweeping the lodge. Widespread in the plains, this
herb is native from Minnesota to Arizona.

1x   Van Bruggen photo

SNOW-ON-THE-MOUNTAIN

Euphorbia marginata   Spurge Family   mid June — Sept.

This showy annual inhabits dry hillsides and prairies.
The upper leaves immediately below the small,
inconspicuous flower clusters have prominently
whitened margins which, when seen from a distance,
cause dense patches of this herb to give a whitish
appearance; hence, its common name. Native from
Minnesota to Montana and south, it is widely
cultivated elsewhere. The stems of most species
of *Euphorbia* have an acrid latex that is
irritating to skin and to linings of intestinal tracts.
Several other alkaloids, not completely understood,
are also present. None appear to have any
beneficial value.

1x   Stockert photo

BUNCHBERRY

Cornus canadensis   Dogwood Family   late June — July

Most members of the Dogwood Family are trees or
shrubs, but this species is a small herb which
springs from an extensive, bulb-like root system, or
rhizome. Stems grow up to 10 inches or more with
four to six leaves forming a circle around each stem.
The flowers are in a small cluster with four whitened
leaves beneath that serve to attract the insects in the
same way as petals. Later, scarlet fruits attract birds
and mammals. Ranging from Greenland to California,
this perennial herb occurs in the Black Hills and in
the Turtle Mountains.

2/3x   Kravig photo

DUCKPOTATO ARROWHEAD
Sagittaria cuneata　Waterplantain Family　late June – Sept.

The tuberous, underground parts of this herbaceous
perennial and other arrowheads were eaten by many
North American Indians. The tubers provided a
welcome change in diet after a long winter when ice
and frozen earth prevented getting most other plant
foods. When cooked, they taste similar to Irish
potatoes. The sexes of the flowers are separate; the
lower ones are female, the upper male. This
photograph shows only male flowers. Arrowheads grow
in shallow water, in potholes, and at the margin
of lakes and slow streams. Waterfowl, especially
diving ducks, feed extensively on the young
shoots and tubers.

1x　Stockert photo

COMMON PEARLY-EVERLASTING
Anaphalis margaritacea　Composite Family　July – Aug.

A conspicuous plant of dry, open prairie and rocky
slopes, this perennial grows up to 2 feet or higher,
with linear (long and narrow) leaves that may be
more than 4 inches long. The leaves and flowers are
wooly-white for most of the growing season, giving
rise to the common name. The flower head has many
dense, pearly-white bracts. After flowering,
whitened hairs aid in seed dispersal. This herb
is quite common in the Black Hills.

1/3x　Kravig photo

CULVERS-ROOT
Veronicastrum virginicum　Snapdragon Family　July – Aug.

The sometimes lavender-tinged blossoms of this
perennial have projecting, needle-like stamens. The
flowers cluster into a long, tapering, distinctive
spike. Stems grow up to 6 feet bearing leaves in
whorls, or circles, with three to six in a whorl. The
juices contain a strong emetic and laxative and were used
as medicine. This herb prefers moist places in
prairie and thickets. Although present from the
eastern half of the Dakotas and Nebraska eastward,
it is rare in the central and western parts of the
northern plains. The origin of the common name
is unknown.

1/3x　Van Bruggen photo

COW PARSNIP

Heracleum sphondylium   Parsley Family   July

A large, perennial weed, this plant
is often found in marshy or rich, damp
soil. The name Cow Parsnip refers to the coarse
and rough appearance of the stems and leaves.
It grows to 6 feet tall. The stem is stout
and has a heavy, branched root system. The
flowers are arranged in large, umbelled
clusters, which are characteristic of the
family. After flowering, the fruits remain on
the branches for several months. They are
flat and heart-shaped with several ribs and
oil tubes lining each face. Cow Parsnip
is common over the northern plains.

1/7x   Van Bruggen photo

MOUNTAIN MEADOWSWEET

Spiraea betulifolia   Rose Family   June – July

Two meadowsweets are found in the northern
plains. This one is not as common as the
other, *S. alba,* which grows in open
meadows and moist prairies. Mountain
Meadowsweet is found, as the name
implies, in mountainous areas of the Black
Hills and west in the Rocky Mountains as
far as British Columbia. A small shrub,
it has woody stems that are often less
than 2 feet tall. The small, white flowers
are in dense clusters at the tops of the
stems. The nectar is very sweet-smelling
and attracts hosts of insects. The term
Spiraea comes from the ancient Greek
word for wreath, hence the term Bridal
Wreath for the commonly cultivated form.

1x   Van Bruggen photo

BALLHEAD ERIOGONUM

Eriogonum pauciflorum   Buckwheat Family   July

Of the dozen or more *Eriogonums*
found in the Great Plains, this and the
Bracted Umbrella Plant (page 15) are
among the ones most commonly encountered.
A drab, gray appearing plant, it has stems
that are short and form dense mats with
most of the leaves at the soil level. The
flowering stalks are almost leafless.
Clusters of very small, white-pink
flowers develop in mid-summer. The deep
root system of the plant allows it to
grow in such inhospitable places as dry,
sandy knolls and clay flats such as are
found in the Badlands.

2/3x   Van Bruggen photo

BROAD-LIPPED TWAYBLADE
Listera convallarioides   Orchid Family   July – Aug.

The pair of roundish, broad leaves about midway
on the stem of this perennial orchid account for
the common name. Intricate flowers, usually
yellowish-green, are arranged in a loose, spike-like
fashion. Plants occasionally have stems taller than
1 foot. The herb grows in damp humus of rich woods
from New England to the Midwest but is restricted
to the Black Hills in the northern plains area. All
orchids should be seen and appreciated in their
native habitat, not picked or transplanted!

1/2x   Kravig photo

WHITE CAMPION
Lychnis alba   Pink Family   July – Aug.

The flowers of White Campion, or White Cockle,
bloom at night when night-flying moths serve as the
principal pollinators. The male and female flowers
are on separate plants; those pictured here are
female. The notched petals radiate above an enlarged
calyx, the whorl of leaves, or sepals, at the base
of the flower. The female flowers mature into capsules
with a toothed opening. A great number of small seeds
are produced. A frequent perennial, possibly biennial,
of roadsides and waste places, this herb grows up to
3 feet. Its range is widespread in Eastern United States.

1/2x   Van Bruggen photo

BOUNCING-BET
Saponaria officinalis   Pink Family   July – Sept.

When Bouncing-bet escapes from cultivation, it
becomes a persisting perennial of roadsides and
waste places, spreading by its roots. The herbs
grow up to 2 feet or more with strictly opposite
leaves. The pinkish-white flowers are borne in
dense clusters on the stem at points where leaves
branch off and at the top of the stem. Typical of the
Pink Family, the petals are notched or lobed. The
generic name, *Saponaria*, refers to the soapy
material, saponin, which is in the stems. Saponin is
poisonous yet animals avoid it because it is
extremely distasteful.

1/2x   Van Bruggen photo

WHORLED MILKWEED

Asclepias verticillata   Milkweed Family   July — Sept.

The white flowers of this herb are smaller than those
of other milkweeds. The normally unbranched stem,
up to 2 feet tall, contains a milky juice which is
poisonous to livestock. The linear leaves are
verticillate, or whorled, which means that several
leaves radiate from a point on the stem. Each leaf
is 1 to 3 inches long. A perennial, it grows in
patches from spreading underground parts. This
milkweed is widely distributed on the plains.

2x   Stockert photo

WESTERN FALSE-BONESET

Kuhnia eupatorioides   Composite Family   July — Oct.

The words *eupatorioides* and "boneset" indicate that
there is some similarity to *Eupatorium*, the Joe-pye-
weeds or true bonesets, (see page 70). This likeness
is seen in the structure of the flower heads which
consist only of tubular florets. The heads of Western
False-boneset are made up of about 30 white to yellow
florets. The herb grow to 3 feet or taller with
several upright branches off the main stem. Leaves
are alternate, not opposite as in the true bonesets.
Ranging from the East Coast to the Rockies and south
to Arizona, this perennial inhabits prairies and
other dry, open places.

1x   Stockert photo

WHITE PRAIRIE ASTER

Aster falcatus   Composite Family   late July — Oct.

Ranging from the Pacific northwest to Nebraska
and the western Dakotas, this perennial is a common
inhabitant of dry prairies. It is recognized by its
flower heads that cluster at the ends and sides
of branches. Each head is about ½ inch across.
Sometimes the ray florets are pink. The leaves are
oblong and about ¾ of an inch long. The herb seldom
grows more than 2 feet high.

2x   Stockert photo

FIELD MINT

Mentha arvensis   Mint Family   July — Aug.

Although grouped in the white flower
section, the flowers of the Common or
Field Mint often vary to rosy-pink. The
very small flowers are sessile, that is,
without stalks, and crowded in the leaf
axils in such a way as to appear to
encircle the stem. The leaves have a strong,
minty odor. Field Mint is very common in
moist or marshy places ranging from Newfoundland to Alaska. The well known plants
Spearmint and Peppermint are also in the
genus *Mentha.* They are found throughout
the United States and Europe. For centuries
they have been cultivated for their essential
oils which are used for flavoring. Indians
used the Field Mint for flavoring, and
they steeped a tea from the leaves and flowers.

3/4x   Van Bruggen photo

SMARTWEED

Polygonum pennsylvanicum   Buckwheat Family   Aug.

The Smartweeds are very common in the
plains. At least 25 species occur in the
northern plains. This one is an ever present
weed in fields and waste places. An annual,
the branched stems often grow to a height of
4 feet. Flowers often are pink, fading to
white as they age. The leaves are lance-shaped
and about 5 inches long. Each plant produces
many seeds each year. Not all germinate
the following year, some remaining dormant
for several years. The Smartweeds are
well known by farmers who are serious in
their weed control efforts.

1/4x   Van Bruggen photo

THIMBLEBERRY

Rubus parviflorus   Rose Family   July — Aug.

A relative of the raspberries and black-
berries, this attractive, shrubby woodland
inhabitant is found on slopes at higher
altitudes in the Black Hills. It ranges in
distribution from Ontario to southern
Alaska. Plants are irregularly branched
and several feet tall. The leaves are
broadly three or five-lobed, often up
to 10 inches across. The white flowers
are about 2 inches across and very showy.
Later in the season, red, raspberry-like
fruits are formed which are ½ / ¾
of an inch in diameter. They taste a little
soapy and are not particularly relished
by wildlife.

1/3x   Van Bruggen photo

BICKNELL GERANIUM

Geranium bicknellii   Geranium Family   Aug.

Typical of the half dozen or so geranium species of the area, this annual or biennial has the characteristic five petals in a symmetrical pattern around a common center. The flowers usually form in pairs in hues from light pink to purple marked with reddish streaks. After flowering, the maturing fruit becomes extended with a beak, hence the use of Cranesbill as another common name. The leaves of the herb are circular in outline with deep incisions. Found in woodlands and thickets, it is also present in the Turtle Mountains of North Dakota and in the Black Hills.

2x   Van Bruggen photo

WHITESTEM EVENING-PRIMROSE

Oenothera nuttallii   Evening-primrose Family   Aug. – Sept.

This perennial has white stems that are so smooth they look as if they were enameled. The flowers are at first white but soon become pink or rose. Each one is about 2 inches across. Plants grow to a height of 2 feet, often branching at the upper part of the main stem. Leaves are oblong and lack the obvious "teeth" so common in other closely related species. The herb spreads by creeping roots in open, flat areas of prairie and can form large, dense patches.

1x   Stockert photo

NODDING LADIES-TRESSES

Spiranthes vernalis   Orchid Family   early Sept.

The nodding, greenish-white flowers of this orchid appear to form a spiral, but close examination reveals that they grow in three rows on a slightly twisted stalk, thus giving the appearance of a spiral. Flower stalks are 20 to 40 inches tall. Two to four stems sprout from a perennial bulb-like root, or rhizome. The leaves are narrow and grow mostly at the base. Growing in bogs or open marshy places in the eastern high plains, this striking rare native herb should be conserved wherever found!

2/3x   Van Bruggen photo

SPREADING PASQUEFLOWER
Anemone patens   Buttercup Family   late Mar. — May

The state flower of South Dakota and one of the earliest on the prairie, Spreading Pasqueflower blooms before surrounding vegetation turns green. The outer parts of the flower, which look like petals, are actually sepals and vary from white to deep lavender. Although the color variance may be caused partly by genetic influences, it is primarily thought to be the result of variable life processes. The long, feathery-tipped fruits suggest the name Prairie-smoke, by which this herbaceous perennial is also called. Spreading Pasqueflower grows throughout the high plains.

1/2x   Stockert photo

Red Flowers

MOUNTAIN WAFER-PARSNIP
Cymopterus montanus   Parsley Family   April — May

One of several wafer-parsnips, or wild parsleys, of the prairie, this herb has a perennial taproot and deeply-cut leaves. The very small, white to purplish flowers form dense umbels, an arrangement which produces a flat to rounded, attractive landing site for insect pollinators. Prairie Indians roasted the roots, then ground them into meal which was baked or made into a thin porridge. It is a common resident on rocky slopes of the Black Hills and the surrounding plains.

1/2x   Stockert photo

MISSOURI MILKVETCH
Astragalus missouriensis   Legume Family   mid April — June

Of the more than 500 species of *Astragalus* that inhabit North America, Missouri Milkvetch is one of the most common. It is characterized by low stems about 4 inches long. The leaflets appear silvery gray due to dense, flattened hairs on the surface. The fruits mature as fleshy pods 3 inches long. Prairie Indians collected various kinds of milkvetch pods for use in soups and other cooking. This perennial herb frequents hills and prairies throughout the northern plains.

1x   Stockert photo

DAMES ROCKET

Hesperis matronalis   Mustard Family   mid April — June

The name *Hesperis*, or "Vesper-flower," was given to this plant over 2,000 years ago for it gives out a lovely perfume only in the evening. The herb was cultivated in Roman gardens by matrons because of its fragrance. Well established in Eastern United States, it persists after cultivation along roadsides and in old gardens in the eastern part of the northern plains. Stems grow from 6 inches to 4 feet tall or more, depending upon available moisture. The flowers are usually deep lavender but may vary to a lighter color. A biennial, it blooms during its second year.

1/3x   Van Bruggen photo

CANADA WILDGINGER

Asarum canadense   Birthwort Family   late April — May

Lacking petals, the flower of this woodland plant has, instead, three brownish-purple sepals which form the showy parts. The flower is borne at the level of the forest litter near the base of the usually paired, heart-shaped leaves. The inside of the flower usually harbors insects who quite accidentally aid in pollination. A common, perennial herb of eastern forests, it occurs infrequently on the loamy slopes of rich woods at the eastern edge of the plains. The horizontal roots, up to ½ inch in diameter, have a ginger-like odor, hence the common name.

1/2x   Van Bruggen photo

PRAIRIE VIOLET

Viola pedatifida   Violet Family   May — June

The most common violet of the high plains, this low perennial is essentially stemless and grows less than 6 inches high. The deeply divided leaves and large, blue to purple flowers distinguish the herb from other blue violets. In all native violets, one of the five petals has a sac-like base which is called a spur. Three of the petals have hairs or beards on the inner surfaces. Several violets, including this one, hybridize freely with other closely related species, making identification of their offspring impossible.

1x   Van Bruggen photo

PURPLESPOT FRITILLARY
Fritillaria atropurpurea Lily Family May – June

The spotted flowers of this perennial account for
another common name, Leopard Lily. The drooping
blossoms are a dull purplish-brown and somewhat
ill-smelling; however, they attract insect pollinators.
The lily-like stems grow up to 2 feet, bearing long,
narrow leaves aligned alternately. Absent in eastern
North and South Dakota, the herb becomes more
frequent westward in the drier prairies. Indians
called it Rice Root because the offshoots and the
scales of the bulb resemble grains of rice.
The bulbs are starchy and good to eat.

1x   Stockert photo

SOUTHERN SHOOTINGSTAR
Dodecatheon pulchellum   Primrose Family   May – June

There are more than 15 species of shootingstar
in temperate North America, ranging from Alaska to
Georgia. This herbaceous perennial is considered to
be cordilleran, meaning "of the mountains," and
occurs in the Black Hills in marshy soil along
streams. Scapes, or leafless stalks, from 6 to 12
inches high, bear pink to purple flowers. The five
petals flare back and the conspicuous, reddish tips
of the stamens form a tight cone which points
downward. The flat, spoon-shaped leaves grow in
a rosette at the base of the plant.

1/2x   Kravig photo

LAMBERT CRAZYWEED
Oxytropis lambertii   Legume Family   May – June

One of a group of plants also called locoweeds,
this stemless herb is toxic to all grazing animals
if enough is eaten. The compound leaves and
flowering scapes, or leafless stalks, arise from a thick
crown at ground level. This is a good way to distinguish
it from *Astragalus* (see pages 37 and 52), a related
genus with which it is often confused. *Astragalus*
has leafy stems with flowers at the tops. Flowers of
Lambert Crazyweed are deep purple but may lighten
as the sun bleaches them. This perennial is one of
several species of *Oxytropis* that are native
to the Great Plains.

1/3x   Stockert photo

STRIPED CORALROOT

Corallorhiza striata   Orchid Family   June

Like all of the coralroots, this one
is dependent on the dead remains of other
plants and fungi in the soil for its nutrition.
Its roots are perennial, and from them
several stems grow to about 15 inches tall.
It forms small, sometimes dense patches
under pines at higher altitudes in the
Black Hills and also in northern North Dakota
in our region. Its distribution in North
America ranges from Quebec to British
Columbia and southward. Prominent purple
stripes on rose-pink flower parts make this
a striking wildflower.

1x   Van Bruggen photo

POINTED PHLOX

Phlox alyssifolia   Phlox Family   May — June

Because of its small size and unusually
showy flowers, this wildflower is particularly
noticed by those who take a close look at
the prairie in the Great Plains during May.
A perennial, this phlox has a short stem
with fibrous, peeling bark. A second
characteristic that distinguishes this
prairie native is the sharp, pointed leaves
with whitened margins. White to rose colored
flowers are usually solitary. Each petal is
about ½ inch long. It grows from western
South Dakota and Nebraska to the
Rocky Mountains.

1½x   Van Bruggen photo

BUFFALOBERRY

Shepherdia argentea   Oleaster Family   May — June

Although May through June is the time of
flowering, this picture was taken in late
July when the Buffaloberry was in full
fruit. The reason that the fruit is pictured
is because this is the only time many people
notice this shrub. The flowers are very small
and dull brown. A perennial shrub, it has
bright green leaves. The stems are 4 to 6
feet tall and become thorny after a year
or so. Buffaloberries were used by Indians
as food throughout the Great Plains. People
still collect them for making jams and jellies.

3/4x   Van Bruggen photo

SHOWY PEAVINE

Lathyrus polymorphus   Legume Family   May — June

Showy Peavine grows 6 to 12 inches tall on weak, straggly stems that have tendrils, the threadlike extensions which help support climbing plants. Four to eight pairs of narrow leaflets make up each compound leaf; their texture varies from smooth to densely hairy. The blue to purplish-red flowers are over 1 inch long. Native to dry, sandy plains of Nebraska, Wyoming, and South Dakota, the perennial herb is principally known for its toxic effect on grazing animals. A disease called lathyrism results when excessive amounts are eaten. Symptoms include a partial paralysis of the limbs.

1/2x   Stockert photo

VIOLET WOODSORREL

Oxalis violacea   Woodsorrel Family   May — June

Widespread in the upland prairie, this inconspicuous herb is often overlooked. A small, stemless perennial, it grows from a deep-seated, brown, scaly bulb about ½ inch in diameter. The leaves have three, heart-shaped segments, typical of the Woodsorrel Family. Flowers, each about ¾ inch across, are on naked stems that are 3 to 5 inches high. *Oxalis* comes from the Greek meaning "sharp" or "bitter" which is the taste of the oxalic acid in the soft, fleshy vegetation. Indian children ate the bulbs and vegetation, giving it the name *Skidadihorit* which means "sour-like-salt."

1x   Van Bruggen photo

SCARLET GAURA

Gaura coccinea   Evening-primrose Family   May — Aug.

These perennials grow up to 18 inches from deep, spreading roots. Leaves are lanceolate to oblong with toothed edges. The narrow flower clusters may be as long as 10 inches. The pink to scarlet, strap-like flower parts resemble honeysuckle blossoms. A covering of white hairs gives this herb a gray appearance, leaving it quite inconspicuous in the dry plains where it is a typical resident.

3x   Stockert photo

BEARBERRY

Arctostaphylos uva-ursi   Heath Family   late May — June

Bearberry, ranging from California to Labrador, is a
low, spreading, woody-stemmed perennial with small,
oval leaves. As is true with many members of the
Heath Family, it is an evergreen. Single plants form a
mat several feet across. The flowers, resembling
small urns, are about ½ inch wide. The bright red,
pea-sized berries need almost a year to mature and,
while not palatable to humans, are reportedly relished
by bears. Indians dried the leaves for smoking.
Bearberry, also called Kinnikinnick, is common in the
Black Hills and in the Turtle Mountains and badlands
of North Dakota.

3/4x   Kravig photo

SHELL-LEAF PENSTEMON

Penstemon grandiflorus   Snapdragon Family   late May — June

Many people of the Great Plains insist that this is
the showiest and most graceful of all prairie plants.
The vegetation is smooth and waxy. Stout, unbranched
stems grow up to 3 feet bearing shell-like leaves
which are sessil (without stalks). The pale
lavender to lilac flowers are 2 inches long or longer.
Prairie Indians prepared extracts of the stems and
roots of this perennial herb to use for treating
fevers and toothaches. Usually found on relatively
undisturbed prairie, it can be successfully transplanted to gardens.

1/2x   Stockert photo

MEADOW ROSE

Rosa blanda   Rose Family   late May — June

The several wild roses in the high plains are hard
to tell apart. At times they crossbreed and produce
hybrids as intermediate forms. Growing up to 30
inches, the stems of this shrub are basically unarmed,
having only a few prickles on new wood. The fragrant
blossoms are usually pink but may vary from white
to deep red. Fruits are called rose hips and become
red when mature in August. They constitute a
valuable winter food for wildlife. An inhabitant of
prairie or prairie remnants along roads, the wild
rose is the state flower of Iowa and North Dakota.

1/3x   Van Bruggen photo

BRACTED SPIDERWORT
Tradescantia bracteata   Spiderwort Family   late May – July

The flowers of this midwestern native vary from pale
pink to deep purple or blue. This color variation
may result from the acidity or alkalinity of the soil
and from genetic differences in the plants. The
short-lived flowers usually close during the heat of
the day and reopen before morning. Growing 1 to 2
feet tall with grassy leaves, this herb prefers moist
habitats such as roadside ditches, railroad embankments, and other open places. Prairie Indians used
the succulent stems as potherbs. This perennial
transplants to gardens very successfully.

2x   Stockert photo

SCARLET GLOBEMALLOW
Sphaeralcea coccinea   Mallow Family   late May – Sept.

This common, showy perennial of sandy, high prairie
soil spreads from creeping roots. The nearly foot-
tall stems bear leaves that are divided into narrow
segments, much like those of its "cousin," Flower-
of-an-hour (see page 21). Branched grayish hairs,
visible only through a hand lens, cover the vegatation.
Creamy-yellow, central, stamen columns vividly accent
the brick-red blossoms. Plains Indians chewed the
mucilages and gums in the stems; they also valued
the herb as a medicine.

1x   Stockert photo

DOWNY PHLOX
Phlox pilosa   Phlox Family   June – July

Downy, or Prairie, Phlox has soft hairs on the stems.
The plants are perennial and grow 1 to 2 feet tall
with opposite, lance-shaped leaves. The flowers,
which are densely clustered at the ends of branches,
are generally in hues from pink to lavender. The
blossoms are tubular below and flare into five limbs
above to a diameter of about an inch. Growing in low
or moist prairie, this herb is found only in the
eastern part of the northern plains where it is
relatively common. Several garden varieties were
adapted from this and other closely related species.

1/2x   Van Bruggen photo

HOUNDS-TONGUE

Cynoglossum officinale   Borage Family   June – July

The common name of this weed of the Great
Plains is a translation of the word *Cynoglossum*
meaning dog and tongue. It refers to the leaves,
which are rough and shaped like a tongue.
Plants are biennial with a flowering stalk
that grows up to 3 feet tall the second year.
The flowers are about ½ inch across with a
dull red color. Later they form a four-parted
nut-like fruit which is covered with small,
hooked bristles. A weed from Europe, it is
found in waste places throughout the
United States.

1/4x   Van Bruggen photo

VENUS' SLIPPER

Calypso bulbosa   Orchid Family   June – July

This is an orchid which is one of a kind.
There is only one species of *Calypso*
and it grows around the world in the north
temperate regions of North America and
Eurasia. Some readily admit it is the most
beautiful of the orchids native to North
America. The single flower is formed at the
tip of a stem about 8 inches tall. Near the
base of the stem there is a single broad
leaf. In our area it grows in cool ravines
of the Black Hills and eastern Wyoming.

1x   Van Bruggen photo

WILD HONEYSUCKLE

Lonicera dioica   Honeysuckle Family   June

Flowers of the Wild Honeysuckle vary in
color from red to yellow on the same plant.
They are clustered at the ends of woody stems
that trail or twine on other plants. Stems
may be up to 6 feet long. Immediately
below the flowers, two broad leaves are
fused together to form a saucer-like base for
the cluster. Lower leaves are ovate and have
a white, waxy covering. Honeysuckle grows
in rich and rocky woodlands throughout the
western parts of Minnesota and Iowa, and west
to the Black Hills.

3/4x   Van Bruggen photo

CLUSTERED BROOMRAPE
Orobanche fasciculata   Broomrape Family   June – July

All broomrapes lack the green pigment, chlorophyll, which is necessary to make their own food. Consequently, they attach themselves to the roots of other plants, particularly sagebrush and wormwood (*Artemisia* sp.). The clustered stems are 3 to 6 inches high with scale-like leaves that have no function and which wither and drop soon after they are formed. Flowers are creamy-white to off-purple, becoming brown towards maturity. The entire plant was used for food by Indians. Common in the high plains, this herbaceous perennial is intriguing to biologists because its method of reproduction is not well understood.

1/3x   Stockert photo

SHOWY MILKWEED
Asclepias speciosa   Milkweed Family   June – July

This perennial is perhaps the most common milkweed of the plains. The herb grows in clumps from creeping roots to a height of at least 3 feet. The rose-pink flowers have specially long "hoods" and "horns." All milkweeds are highly specialized for insect pollination with the pollen massed into sharp, forked devices. These masses are removed when an insect's leg accidentally becomes lodged in the sharp angle. Small insects whose legs become trapped often die there because they cannot remove the pollen masses. Early settlers collected the downy seeds and used them for stuffing pillows and mattresses.

1x   Stockert photo

BLUE VERBENA
Verbena hastata   Verbena Family   June – Aug.

The erect stem of this slender verbena has several branches along the upper portion. Quarter-inch, lavender flowers form dense, narrow spikes that mature into seed pods. The lance-shaped leaves have sharply toothed margins. Growing up to 5 feet, this perennial prefers open, moist places throughout Canada and the United States. Some people believed that because the juice of this plant was ill-tasting it had to have some beneficial action. Consequently, it has long been used as a medicine. The verbenas, also called vervains, were considered sacred herbs in ancient Rome and were used in processions and ceremonies.

1/3x   Van Bruggen photo

PURPLE PRAIRIECLOVER

Petalostemum purpureum   Legume Family   June — Sept.

The small flowers of this perennial are only ¼ inch
long and are red, usually not purple as the name
suggests. The leaf segments are narrower than those
of White Prairieclover (see page 45). The vegetation
is fragrant when bruised or shredded. Prairie Indians
prepared a tea by steeping the dried leaves of both
this plant and White Prairieclover. They also chewed
the inner portions of the deep, spreading roots.
This herb produces a binding effect on bowels. It is
a native throughout most of the Great Plains.

1x   Van Bruggen photo

ROCKY MOUNTAIN BEEPLANT

Cleome serrulata   Caper Family   June — Sept.

The young, tender shoots and leaves of this annual
were eaten by western Indians. They also boiled the
stems until a black residue remained. They used this
as a paint or dye, or dried it to use later as food.
The flowers have individual stems and several long
stamens which extend up to an inch beyond the
blossom. They attract a number of insects, including
bees. The herb sometimes reaches a height of more
than four feet and frequently grows in sandy soil
throughout the plains states.

1/7x   Stockert photo

RUSH SKELETON-PLANT

Lygodesmia juncea   Composite Family   June — Oct.

Usually five white to pink florets make up each
flower head. The nearly leafless, herbaceous stems
branch from the base and grow to less than 2 feet
tall. They appear as inconspicuous, greenish-gray
skeletons when not in flower. A deep, spreading
root system adapts this perennial to its dry prairie
habitat. Several kinds of insects lay eggs in the stem
which cause the formation of hazelnut-sized galls.
Dakota and Nebraska Indians soaked the stems and
used the infusion to bathe sore eyes. Indian mothers
also drank the mixture to increase the flow of
milk for nursing.

1x   Van Bruggen photo

SULLIVANT MILKWEED
Asclepias sullivantii   Milkweed Family   late June – July

A showy perennial of low, moist prairies, this herb
can be distinguished from most other milkweeds by
its smooth, shiny leaves. Nevertheless, it is often
confused with Common Milkweed (*A. syriaca*).
Sullivant Milkweed, however, does not occur in weedy
or disturbed places as does the other. The species
pictured here with light lavender to purple flowers
is sensitive to grazing and is a true prairie
inhabitant. The fruits, called follicles, remain
erect at maturity and contain many flat, silky seeds.

1/3x   Van Bruggen photo

PALE PURPLE-CONEFLOWER
Echinacea angustifolia   Composite Family   late June – July

One of the prominent sentinels of prairie knolls in
the northern plains, this herb transplants very
successfully and makes an attractive border in
gardens. The outer ray florets of the flower head
are rose-purple and usually drooping. The dome-like
center consists of disk florets and pointed
bracts of equal length. These bracts remain for
months after the seeds have been dispersed. Stems
grow from 1 to 2 feet tall bearing few lanceolate
leaves. A hardy perennial, it has rough, blackened
rootstocks that Prairie Indians used for medicine.

1/2x   Van Bruggen photo

WOOLLY VERBENA
Verbena stricta   Verbena Family   late June – Sept.

The flowers of this herb are less than ½ inch across
and are usually lavender but may vary from white to
deep purple. The blossoms form a long, fleshy spike,
blooming from the bottom up. The stout stems cluster
in groups and grow 2 to 4 feet tall. Coarse hairs
cover the leaf and stem surfaces. Occurring in fields
and prairies, this verbena's deep root system gives
it the ability to resist drought. Native in Central
United States and Canada, this perennial has spread
eastward. Grazing animals avoid it because of its
bitter juice. Vervain is another name for verbena.

1/3x   Van Bruggen photo

WAVYLEAF THISTLE

Cirsium undulatum   Composite Family   late June — Sept.

A native herb of the western plains, this thistle is often confused with Flodman Thistle (see page 66). However, Wavyleaf Thistle has a tendency to grow in patches and has thicker stems. The flower heads are also larger, commonly 2 to 2½ inches in diameter. Although both kinds overlap in their distribution, they are considered to be biologically distinct species. A true prairie inhabitant, Wavyleaf Thistle is a biennial and prefers well drained sites. It ranges to the foothills of the Rocky Mountains.

1/2x   Stockert photo

MARSH HEDGE-NETTLE

Stachys palustris   Mint Family   July

Typical of the Mint Family, the flowers of this perennial are highly specialized for pollination by insects. The blossoms have a two-lobed, upper lip and a longer, three-lobed, lower lip which serves as a convenient landing site for insects. *Stachys*, meaning "spike," refers to the arrangement of the flowers on the stem. The hairy leaves shaped like those of the common nettle (*Urtica* sp.) account for the name but, unlike the true nettle, the hairs do not sting. This wide-ranging herb grows in moist areas of the prairie and open places in alluvial woods.

1/2x   Van Bruggen photo

BUTTERFLY MILKWEED

Asclepias tuberosa   Milkweed Family   July

One of the showiest of all moist prairie plants within the eastern part of the northern plains, this striking perennial provides a sharp contrast to green surroundings with its reddish-orange flowers. The lance-shaped leaves, 2 to 4 inches long, are softly hairy. Unlike other milkweeds, it does not have milky juice in its stems. Because of its color and odor, the herb attracts many insects, including butterflies. Indians collected the tuberous roots and cooked them for food or ate them raw when used as a medicine.

1/2x   Stockert photo

SWAMP MILKWEED
Asclepias incarnata   Milkweed Family   July

There are at least 20 species of milkweeds
that are wide-spread in the Great Plains.
This is the only species of our region that
is restricted to swampy or marshy places.
A perennial, it has smooth stems about
3 feet tall and long, lance-shaped leaves
The flower clusters are rose to crimson red
in color. After flowering, slender fruits
are produced in pairs that are about 3 inches
long and tapered at each end. Swamp Milkweed
is more common in the eastern part of the
northern plains.

2/3x   Van Bruggen photo

MOUNTAIN THISTLE
Cirsium drummondii   Composite Family   July – Aug.

The Black Hills of South Dakota is perhaps
as far east as this thistle is found. It is
native in meadows and valleys of mountainous
regions in the northern and western parts of
the United States and Canada. Usually rose or
pink in color, the head is sometimes white.
The stems are short, not more than 18 inches
tall, but thick and watery. The long leaves,
with many pinnate divisions that are spine
pointed, make this thistle easy to recognize
in the field. Like a number of the prairie
thistles, it is not a weed.

1/3x   Van Bruggen photo

WOOD SAGE
Teucrium canadense   Mint Family   July – Aug.

This mint has a flower structure unlike
any other in the family. Typical of all the
mints, the petals are fused and highly
modified for insect pollination. However,
the upper lip is only partly developed and
reduced to small, horn-like projections on
each side. The stamen filaments extend and
arch over the large, lower lip that acts
as a "landing strip" for insects. Wood
Sage, which is also called Germander, grows
in wood thickets throughout the northern
plains. Plants are up to 3 feet tall with
large, lance-shaped leaves. The flowers are
arranged in a terminal spike.

3/4x   Van Bruggen photo

WOOD LILY

Lilium philadelphicum   Lily Family   July

An inhabitant of woodlands and thickets from Maine
to British Columbia, this perennial occurs in moist
prairie areas of the high plains. The unbranched
stems grow up to 2 feet from a white, scaly bulb
that is edible. The narrow leaves are arranged in
circles, or whorls, with three to six leaves in a
whorl. There may be up to three, reddish-orange
flowers that are erect and very showy. Purple spots
decorate the bases of the petals on the inside. This
herb has western varieties that are deep red.

1/3x   Kellogg photo

CANADA TICKCLOVER

Desmodium canadense   Legume Family   July — Aug.

Tickclovers have segmented fruiting pods with tiny,
hooked hairs that cling to clothing, fur, and other
soft material. Widespread in the East, a number of
species range into the western plains, this one
being perhaps the most common. This perennial
inhabits moist areas, edges of thickets, and open
woods. The herb grows erect reaching a height of 4
or 5 feet with several flowering branches. The leaves
are composed of three leaflets with the terminal
one larger than the two lateral ones. The flowers,
which darken toward maturity, develop into nutritious
seeds which are eaten by upland birdlife.

1/2x   Van Bruggen photo

SPOTTED CORALROOT

Corallorhiza maculata   Orchid Family   July — Aug.

A perennial, this orchid lacks green tissues and is
therefore a true saprophyte. It obtains its
nutrition from the close association its roots have
with fungi called mycorhizae which live in the humus
of the forest floor. The less-than-12-inch stems are
fleshy with leaves reduced to scales. Flowers are
brownish-white with purple spots. Though orchids are
usually rare, this herb is frequently seen in rich woods
from Newfoundland to the West Coast, including
the Black Hills. Orchids should not be transplanted
because most are rare and their natural habitat
cannot be duplicated in cultivation.

2/3x   Kravig photo

LONGTUBE TWINFLOWER
Linnaea borealis Honeysuckle Family July – Aug.

This plant was named after the great Swedish botanist, Linnaeus. The small, funnel-shaped flowers are slightly more than ½ inch long. Typical of most members of the Honeysuckle Family, the flowers are in pairs at the ends of slender, 3 to 6 inch stalks. These stalks and the nearly oval, evergreen leaves, about 1 inch long, grow from short, branched stems which rise from a larger, trailing stem. This woody-base herb inhabits woods and bogs in northern latitudes of the United States and in Canada. It is quite common in the Black Hills.

2x Kravig photo

THREE-NERVE FLEABANE
Erigeron subtrinervis Composite Family July – Aug.

This herb is common in the Black Hills and in the Rocky Mountains but is rare in western North Dakota. It inhabits open woodlands and other semi-shaded places. The stems, 1 to 2 feet tall, sprout from a perennial, creeping, bulb-like root, or rhizome. The leaves have three, prominent nerves extending into the blades from the leaf base, hence, its common name. Bright pink flower heads up to 2 inches across make it a showy plant when in bloom. Several closely related species are cultivated in Western United States.

1x Van Bruggen photo

FLODMAN THISTLE
Cirsium flodmani Composite Family July – Aug.

A true member of the prairie, this thistle is usually found in poorly drained soils. After spreading by creeping rootstocks that are short lived, the plant produces a stout taproot and grows about 2 feet high. The spine-pointed leaves are covered by dense, white, woolly hairs. The flower heads are made up of tubular florets varying from rose to deep lavender. When in bloom, bumblebees are important insect visitors. Contrary to several other thistles, this biennial herb is a native of the plains.

1x Van Bruggen photo

WOODLAND PINEDROPS

Pterospora andromeda   Heath Family   July — Aug.

The unbranched stems of this perennial grow from
the humus and underground parts of pines and other
conifers. The herb lacks chlorophyll, hence it is
called a saprophyte. Leaves are scale-like and not
functional. The brownish-yellow flowers bloom along
the upper part of the stem, each curved downward.
After flowering, the fleshy stems remain as dried
fibrous stalks for a year or more. Plants commonly
reach 3 feet tall and in this area grow under
pines in western South Dakota.

1x   Van Bruggen photo

THICKSPIKE GAYFEATHER

Liatris pycnostachya   Composite Family   July — Aug.

This tall gayfeather inhabits moist areas of the
plains or roadside prairie remnants. Widespread in
the eastern plains, it does occur westward in the
eastern parts of the Dakotas and Nebraska. The stems
are flexible and unbranched; many narrow leaves grow
along the stem up to the flower heads. It is commonly
over 3 feet tall when in flower. The heads are
arranged in a dense spike, flowering in sequence
from the top down. With some care, it can be
successfully transplanted to gardens. Several
horticultural forms similar to this perennial herb
are cultivated as ornamentals.

1x   Van Bruggen photo

SWAMP SMARTWEED

Polygonum coccineum   Buckwheat Family   July — Sept.

Many swamps and shallow ponds in the pothole region
of the high plains may be covered with this herb which
spreads by rhizomes, or bulb-like roots. Stems,
which reach 2 to 3 feet high, inflate when growing
in water. They bear oval leaves up to 6 inches long.
Indians collected rhizomes of several kinds of
smartweeds and ate them either raw or roasted.
They have a nutty flavor and are nutritious.
This perennial plant is valuable for retaining the
vegetative cover for wildlife in marshy areas.

3/4x   Van Bruggen photo

FIREWEED

Epilobium angustifolium   Evening-primrose Family   July – Sept.

This tall perennial is one of the first invaders
of disturbed soil. In a forest which has been cut
through by a road or destroyed by fire, it will be
seen for several summers thereafter. Mountain
meadows are ablaze with color when Fireweed is
blooming. Inhabiting high latitudes across North
America, the herb is common in the Black Hills
though infrequent in eastern North Dakota. The
rose-magenta flowers are inferior, meaning that the
ovary is below the flowering parts. The ovary
develops a slender pod, or capsule, containing many
seeds, each with a tuft of hairs for easy distribution.

1/2x   Van Bruggen photo

HOARY ASTER

Mackeranthera canescens Composite Family   July – Oct.

White hairs covering the leaves and stems of this
plant account for its common name. A biennial,
usually less than a foot tall, it is a common herb
of dry prairie, especially in the western part. The
leaves are linear to lanceolate and are more numerous
on the lower part of the stem. The color of the ¾-
inch-wide flower heads varies around bluish-purple.
When in bloom, the plant is particularly showy on
dry clayish slopes.

1x   Stockert photo

BUSH MORNING-GLORY

Ipomoea leptophylla Morning-glory Family   late July – Sept.

A frequent herb of dry prairie, Bush Morning-glory
has several, many-leaved branches that grow up to
3 feet in height and 4 to 6 feet in width at the base.
In the early morning hours during its blooming
season, the bush may be covered with large, funnelform
flowers. It grows from an unbelievable large taproot
that may be over 18 inches in diameter at the top
and up to 4 feet long! When under 5 years old, the
root is not woody and is quite palatable; it served
as a food source for the Plains Indians.

1/2x   Stockert photo

COMMON BURDOCK

Arctium minus   Composite Family   Aug. – Sept.

A troublesome herb of overgrazed pastures and open,
wooded draws, this biennial is more abundant in the
eastern prairie. The first year it produces large
leaves at the base of the stem; these leaves resemble
those of rhubarb but are narrower and hairy. A
single, stout flowering stalk appears the second year,
growing up to 3 feet or more.The rose-purple flower
heads have hook-tipped bracts which later dry and form
a bur that catches on clothes or fur, consequently
distributing the enclosed seeds. The Omaha Indians
used the roots as a medicine for pleurisy.

1x   Van Bruggen photo

SILKY ASTER

Aster sericeus   Composite Family   Aug. – Sept.

The oblong leaves of this perennial have long,
silvery hairs which press close to the surface,
making it a striking plant even before flowering.
The stems branch irregularly near the base and seldom
grow higher than 18 inches. Each flower head is just
over an inch across with 15 to 30 lavender rays and a
yellow center. Silky Aster is typically an herb
of rich prairie remnants in the eastern area of the
Dakotas and is even more common in Nebraska and
western Iowa.

1/2x   Van Bruggen photo

SISKIYOU ASTER

Aster hesperius   Composite Family   Aug. – Sept.

This aster is frequently seen along stream banks and
in open ravines at higher elevations. It ranges from
Canada to Missouri, including the Black Hills where
it grows up to 3 feet. The perennial herb spreads by
creeping rhizomes, or bulb-like roots. Flowers vary
from light pink to light blue. The principal leaves
are lance-shaped, about 4 inches long. It transplants
to gardens quite successfully providing a showy
display of flowers.

1/2x   Van Bruggen photo

SPOTTED JOE-PYE-WEED

Eupatorium maculatum Composite Family Aug. – Sept.

The tapering leaves of this perennial are arranged
in circles of four to six leaves with each circle
at a various point on the stem. Its purple-spotted
stems grow to 3 feet tall from a stout, fibrous
root. Pink to purple flower clusters form a flat to
rounded top that is very showy. The herb inhabits
open, swampy places, often along streams. Native in
moist places from Newfoundland to British Columbia,
it ranges as far south as Nebraska. Although rare or
lacking in western North Dakota, it is frequently
seen elsewhere in the northern plains.

1/2x   Van Bruggen photo

DOTTED GAYFEATHER

Liatris punctata Composite Family Aug. – Oct.

Found in dry or sandy prairie in the high plains,
this herb produces pink to purple flower heads, each
about ½ inch across, that form a dense spike. Each
head has six to nine florets. Several stiff, narrow stems
grow up to 2 feet from a lemon-sized underground
corm, a solid bulb-like root. Plains Indians ate the
corms, but only as a survival food for these
perennial roots are coarse and fibrous, and not
very nutritious.

2/3x   Van Bruggen photo

ROCKY MOUNTAIN GAYFEATHER

Liatris ligulistylis Composite Family Aug. – Sept.

This perennial herb, also called Blazingstar,
has purple flower heads that are larger than other
gayfeather species. It also has long styles (the
slender stalk of the central pistil) which project
from the individual florets. Stems grow 4 feet tall
from a hard, swollen base called a corm. There may
be as many as 75 leaves on each plant. Very showy
in moist prairie or damp soil along streams, it is
native in all of the northern plains states. In the
Black Hills it is particularly vivid in meadows.

2/3x   Van Bruggen photo

WESTERN IRONWEED

Vernonia fasciculata   Composite Family   Aug. – Sept.

This perennial has tough, wiry stems which sprout in clusters from a heavy root system. These stems grow 2 to 6 feet tall bearing narrow, sharply toothed leaves that are dotted by small pits on the undersides. Each flower head has 10 or more small, symmetrical, reddish-purple florets. These blossoms mature into hairy seeds which slowly turn dull brown before dropping. Preferring moist or low places in prairie or roadside ditches, this herb is rare in the western parts of the Dakotas and Nebraska.

2/3x   Van Bruggen photo

ROUNDHEAD BUSHCLOVER

Lespedeza capitata   Legume Family   Aug. – Sept.

The creamy-white flowers of this open prairie perennial cluster into a dense head; however, they are nearly hidden by the bracts, or modified leaves associated with the flower. These bracts soon turn a rich brown, as shown here, making the flower heads very showy. Slender, flexible stems, crowded with many three-parted leaves, grow up to 3 feet. Dakota Indians cut the stems into small pieces and burned them close to the skin as a relief for rheumatism and neuralgia. Most bushclovers offer nutritious and palatable grazing for livestock and a food source of seeds for upland birds.

1x   Van Bruggen photo

NEW ENGLAND ASTER

Aster novae-angliae   Composite Family   Sept.

One of the most striking of all the asters, this perennial occurs from New England to the eastern part of the Great Plains. The stout stem commonly grows to 5 feet and branches at the top. Numerous hairy leaves clasp the stem. The ray florets vary from light rose to deep purple. This herb prefers a moist habitat, such as alluvial woods along streams. It is easily transplanted and does well as a garden border.

2/3x   Van Bruggen photo

NARROWLEAF PENSTEMON

Penstemon angustifolius   Snapdragon Family
May – June

The azure flowers of Narrowleaf Penstemon form at the top of usually curved stems. Occasionally several flowers on a plant may be pink or lighter than the usual blue. Most plants are not more than a foot tall, growing in clusters from a woody, perennial base. Leaves are 2 to 3 inches long, sessile (without stalks), and covered with a waxy surface. A native of the western plains, Indians used the roots of this herb for medicine.

2x   Stockert photo

Blue Flowers

LANCELEAF BLUEBELLS

Mertensia lanceolata   Borage Family   mid April – June

This prairie herb has deep blue flowers that cluster on one side at the top of semi-arching stems that are 6 to 10 inches long. Each blossom is ½ inch long. The leaves and stems are smooth and white-waxy, without hairs. Leaves are lance-shaped, 2 to 4 inches long. The plant has a stout, perennial root which, if carefully removed, can be successfully transplanted to gardens. Although not abundant in any particular place, it is scattered throughout dry and sandy prairies in the northern plains.

1x   Stockert photo

ROCKY MOUNTAIN IRIS

Iris missouriensis   Iris Family   May – June

Sometimes called Blue Flag, this meadow perennial ranges from western North Dakota, south to Nebraska, and west to California. It is common in meadows of the Black Hills. The flowers are usually pale lavender but may be much darker or lighter. Stems grow up to 2 feet from a branched rhizome system. The rootstocks contain a bitter, resinous substance reported to be poisonous to livestock. Most likely the Plains Indians carefully avoided it. The herb can be easily transplanted to gardens.

1/7x   Stockert photo

COMMON BLUE-EYED-GRASS
Sisyrinchium montanum   Iris Family   May – June

Except when blooming, this herb is very inconspicuous because of its grass-like leaves and narrow-winged stems. The six-parted flowers grow in small clusters from the stem. Each cluster is enveloped at its base by 2 bracts, or modified leaves, like the common garden iris. Three-celled, berry-shaped pods only ¼ inch wide develop after flowering, each containing several seeds. This perennial has fibrous roots and short rhizomes (thick underground stems) typical of the Iris Family. It is common in moist meadows in the temperate part of the United States.

3x   Stockert photo

AMERICAN VETCH
Vicia americana   Legume Family   May – June

The common vetch of the prairies, this herb has eight or more small leaf segments of which the uppermost pair is modified into climbing tendrils. The stems are weak and straggling, occasionally reaching 3 feet long. They often climb more robust plants. The rose, or purple to blue, flowers are up to an inch long on short stalks. A valuable forage plant, Plains Indians also savored it. They prepared the tender, young stems and seeds in a variety of ways. This perennial is a native of temperate North America and is common in thickets, moist meadows, and prairie grasslands.

1/2x   Van Bruggen photo

PRAIRIE TURNIP
Psoralea esculenta   Legume Family   May – July

Called Tipsin by the Dakota Indians and Indian-turnip by early settlers, this perennial has roots which were an important food of plains inhabitants. In summer the 3 to 4 inch tuberous roots were peeled and stored so that they could be ground and pounded, providing a starchy meal. Plants are a foot high, much branched from the base, with flowers arranged in short, dense spikes. A small pod containing a pea-like seed forms later in the season. This herb is common on the northern prairies.

1x   Stockert photo

BLUE FLAX
Linum perenne   Flax Family   June – July

Blue Flax is a perennial herb that occurs
in Europe and America. For years the American
form was thought to be a different species.
The stems are branched and about 10 inches
tall. Its leaves are narrow. Because of the
slender nature of the stems and leaves,
it is largely unnoticed until it flowers.
Then each branch ending is covered with
broad, five-petalled flowers that make the
plant very showy. Blue Flax is relatively
common on hills and eroded banks over the
northern plains.

1x   Van Bruggen photo

LUPINE
Lupinus argenteus   Legume Family   June – July

Of the many native lupines of the Great
Plains, the Rocky Mountains, and on west, two
are found in the western part of the northern
plains and the Black Hills. This is the more
common of the two. It is a perennial with a
single stem or occasionally a branched one.
Leaves are palmately divided with five to
nine or more narrow segments. Blue to lavender
flowers are produced in spikes at the ends
of upper branches. As the flowers mature,
the stem elongates to as much as three times
its original length. It is found in meadows
and open woods from the central Dakotas
and Nebraska westward.

1/3x   Van Bruggen photo

LONG-SPUR VOILET
Viola adunca   Violet Family   June

As a group, the violets are notoriously
difficult to distinguish with any degree
of certainty. However, the Long-Spur Violet
is an exception. A woodland violet, it has
a short, above-ground stem with several heart-
shaped leaves. At the base of each leaf stalk
there are a pair of small bracts called stipules.
These have prominent teeth at their ends.
This characteristic, along with the unusually
long spurs of the flowers, makes this violet
easy to identify. In our area it grows from
eastern North Dakota west to the Rocky
Mountains.

1/2x   Van Bruggen photo

LEADPLANT

Amorpha canescens   Legume Family   June – Aug.

The leaden-gray leaves account for the common name.
A very dense layer of short hairs covers the small,
oval leaflets, masking the green color. The small,
usually dark lavender flowers consist of a single,
prominent petal and lack the keel (like the keel of
a boat) and wings so typical of legume flowers.
Leadplant, a deep-rooted, low shrub of the entire
North American prairie, is palatable and nutritious to
livestock. Prairie Indians stripped the leaves to make
a hot, tea-like drink.

1/2x   Van Bruggen photo

SAWSEPAL PENSTEMON

Penstemon glaber   Snapdragon Family   June – July

The common name derives from the sawtoothed lobes
of the sepals at the outer base of each flower.
Glaber is from the same word root as "glabrous,"
meaning "smooth;" it refers to the waxy leaf
surfaces. Stems of this herb are 1 to 2 feet high.
Flowers are a rich blue and more than an inch long.
A perennial of dry prairies, it is native from
North Dakota to Nebraska in most of the high plains
region except the eastern part.

1x   Stockert photo

SLENDER PENSTEMON

Penstemon gracilis   Snapdragon Family   mid June – July

This later blooming penstemon has slender stems up
to 18 inches tall. Each plant has three to five pairs
of opposite leaves that are 2 to 4 inches long.
The pale pink to light blue flowers are almost an
inch long and are usually on short stems that grow
from the axils of the upper leaves. After the petals
drop in August and September, the maturing fruit
capsules make the plant more conspicuous. Very
common on dry and sandy prairie, this perennial herb
is native from Canada to New Mexico and east to
Wisconsin.

2x   Stockert photo

ALPINE HEDYSARUM
Hedysarum alpinum   Legume Family   July

A number of wildflowers occur in the northern
plains, especially at higher altitudes of
the Black Hills, which are called boreal
species. They are centrally native to regions
which have colder climates — those closer to
the Artic Circle. At upper altitudes of the
Black Hills this relatively inconspicuous
plant may be found in rocky soil under pines.
A perennial, the stem has a number of compound
leaves, each with 11 to 21 or more ovate leaflets.
The flower stalks are wand-like, with individual
flowers arranged in a row on one side of the stalk.
The petals are mostly lavender with occasional
streaks of white.

3/4x   Van Bruggen photo

SKULLCAP
Scutellaria galericulata   Mint Family   July

The Skullcaps are widely spread throughout
North America as well as in the Old World.
In the northern plains there are three
species which are found in moist woods or
thickets. The common name is derived from
a translation of the Greek word *galerum*,
which was a skullcap worn by the Romans.
This mint is a perennial, growing from
creeping stems. The blue to lavender flowers
grow singly in the axils of opposite leaves,
giving the appearance that they are paired.
The petal parts are about one inch long
and fused together to give a structure
highly specialized for insect pollination.

1x   Van Bruggen photo

VENUS' LOOKING GLASS
Triodanis leptocarpa   Bluebell Family   July

The very narrow stems and leaves make
this member of the bluebell family very
obscure on the prairie. Flowers form
along the upper part of the stem in the
leaf axils. They are less than ½ inch
across, usually blue or fading to
lavender. The plants are annuals and grow
from seed each year. The common name
alludes to the shiny and polished
appearance of the flat seeds that look
like small mirrors. Venus' Looking Glass
is one of two members of the *Triodanis*
group that are found in the Great
Plains.

3/4x   Van Bruggen photo

COMMON CHICORY

Cichorium intybus   Composite Family   July

Originally a native of Europe, chicory
is now a naturalized weed of roadsides
and waste places in most of North America.
It grows from a deep, perennial taproot.
The stems are almost skeleton-like because
of the irregular branching and the scarcity
of leaves. A close look at the delicate
flower head reveals that each flower unit
is a ray flower. In other words, there is
no central disk of flowers as in many of
the Composite group. The common name comes
from the European use of the root as
flavoring for coffee.

1x   Van Bruggen photo

PURPLE VIRGIN'S BOWER

Clematis tenuiloba   Buttercup Family   July

Most of the virgin's bowers are climbing
vines that grow up and trail over the lower
limbs of trees in wooded areas. This one
is of small stature and on occasion will
climb but is usually matted or sprawled
over rocks in wooded places in the Black
Hills and west to the Rocky Mountains. The
leaves are three-parted and then sub-
divided again. Deep purple flowers are
solitary on stalks about 6 inches tall.
The four, thin, strap-shaped, petal-like
structures are actually colored sepals.
A number of *Clematis* species are
cultivated as perennials.

1/3x   Van Bruggen photo

DRAGONHEAD

Dracocephalum parviflorum   Mint Family   July

An imported weed from Asia, Dragonhead
is a biennial found throughout the United
States. The stems are erect with few
branches. Its leaves are lance-shaped and
spine-tipped. Flowers are produced in a
dense, almost head-like cluster with many
spiny bracts. They are nearly obscured by
the spine-tipped and toothed leaves. The
shape of the flower suggested the Greek
name *Dracocephalum*, which means Dragonhead. This plant does not have as strong
an odor as found in many mints.

1x   Van Bruggen photo

MONK'S HOOD

Aconitum columbianum   Buttercup Family   July — Aug.

Wherever they occur, Monk's Hoods are relatively uncommon in terms of numbers. They usually grow in special habitats requiring certain soil types, along with specific amounts of moisture and shade. This one is found in the Black Hills and southwest to Colorado and the Rocky Mountains. The flower has a highly arched and purple colored sepal called the helmet. This results in a hollow crown. The opening of the flower is narrow and almost beak-like. Plants are one to two feet tall with several deeply divided "crowfeet-like" leaves. The plants, especially the seeds and underground parts, are very poisonous. The toxic alkaloid is called aconitine.

1/2x   Van Bruggen photo

ARROW-LEAVED ASTER

Aster sagittifolius   Composite Family   July — Aug.

To the not-so-careful observer, it may seem that the number of asters is very large. They are a difficult group to completely understand, but have enough individual differences so that identification is possible. There are over 20 species in the northern plains. This one is found in the eastern parts of the Dakotas and Nebraska and on south. The leaves are conspicuously arrow-shaped, which is the meaning of the word *sagittifolius*. The purple to blue flowers are produced in a loose spike on stems that may be 4 feet tall. It grows in dry and moist thickets or in woods.

1x   Van Bruggen photo

BLUEBELL

Campanula rotundifolia   Bluebell Family   July — Aug.

A number of common names are applied to this Bluebell, including Harebell and Bluebells-of-Scotland. It grows throughout North America as well as in the Old World. The bell-shaped flowers are distinctive of the family. Plants are perennial with clumps of stems that reach to 12 inches or more. The basal leaves are rounded, hence the term *rotundifolia*, but the upper stem leaves are narrow and linear. It grows on a variety of soils in both meadows and woods in the northern plains and in the Black Hills.

1x   Van Bruggen photo

BLUE LETTUCE

Lactuca oblongifolia   Composite Family   late June — Aug.

The blossoms of all the wild lettuces consist of ray florets, each with a single, strap-shaped petal. The flower heads of this one are very similar to Common Chicory *(Cichorium intybus)*, a composite with blue blossoms common in the Eastern United States. *Lactuca* comes from the Greek word meaning "milk." It refers to the milky latex contained within the smooth, waxy stems of this perennial. Leaves are alternate and more narrowly lobed than other lettuces. Common on roadsides and in waste places, it may grow up to 4 feet. This herb is persistent but not particularly objectionable.

1x   Van Bruggen photo

PALESPIKE LOBELIA

Lobelia spicata   Bluebell Family   July — Aug.

This perennial, smaller than most other lobelias, has bluish-white flowers that are less than ½ inch long. The herb is slender, usually less than 18 inches high, with oblong leaves. It grows in moist, open areas but remains almost unnoticed among the prairie grasses because of its small flowers and stature. Sensitive to grazing and mowing, it quickly disappears if its prairie habitat is disturbed. Several varieties of this species are found throughout eastern North America.

2x   Van Bruggen photo

TALL BELLFLOWER

Campanula americana   Bellflower Family   Aug.

Tall, or American, Bellflower has bluish-lavender flowers that are shallow. Most other native bell-flowers are more bell-shaped. The flowers each slightly exceed 1 inch in diameter and are borne along the stem in a spike-like, yet broadly curved fashion. Bellflowers are closely related to the sunflowers; the main difference between them is that sunflowers have many, small flowers called florets in each flower head whereas bellflowers do not have florets. These annual herbs grow in alluvial or moist thickets in the eastern part of the plains where the prairies give way to the forests.

3/4x   Van Bruggen photo

BIGBLUE LOBELIA
Lobelia siphilitica   Bluebell Family   Aug. — Sept.

The deep blue flowers of this herb, which are
highly adapted for insect pollination, are arranged
in a terminal spike upon a stout, unbranched stem.
Leaves are in the shape of lance heads. The Indians
used the leaves of closely related species for
making tobacco. They probably used several species
for medicinal purposes as well. Bigblue Lobelia was
used for the treatment of syphilis and had little or
no effectiveness. A variety of alkaloids have been
isolated from most American species of lobelia,
several closely related to nicotine. This perennial is
common in moist, open areas along lakes and streams.

1x   Van Bruggen photo

AROMATIC ASTER
Aster oblongifolius   Composite Family   late Aug. — Sept.

Occurring on dry, sunny slopes throughout the
northern plains, this perennial is a good indicator
of prairie that has had little or no domestic
grazing or mowing. Short, oblong leaves grow from
the stem which branches near the base forming a wide,
low outline. The flower heads are up to 1 inch in
diameter; rays vary from pink to purple. The
herb is easily cultivated in gardens, requiring
no extra water.

1/2x   Van Bruggen photo

DOWNY GENTIAN
Gentiana puberulenta   Gentian Family   early Sept.

One of the really beautiful wildflowers of the true
prairie, Downy Gentian, sometimes called Prairie
Gentian, is perennial with erect, clustered stems
that grow up to 2 feet. The deep bluish-purple
flowers which are grouped at the top of the stem
have plaits, or folds, between the corolla lobes.
This herb ranges from the East Coast to eastern
North and South Dakota. When it is found in the
prairie, it is an indication that the area has had
little grazing or disturbance of any kind.

1x   Van Bruggen photo

INDEX